Ceritalah

Ceritalah
MALAYSIA IN TRANSITION

KARIM RASLAN

TIMES BOOKS INTERNATIONAL
Singapore • Kuala Lumpur

Front cover photo of Karim Raslan by
Tara Sosrowardoyo
Photo of Kuala Lumpur on page 88 by V. Chantiran

Cover design by Hikayat Media, Kuala Lumpur

© 1996 Times Editions Pte Ltd
Reprinted 1996 (twice)

Published by Times Books International
an imprint of Times Editions Pte Ltd
Times Centre
1 New Industrial Road
Singapore 536196
Fax: (65) 2854871 Tel: (65) 2848844
e-mail: te@corp.tpl.com.sg

Times Subang
Lot 46, Subang Hi-Tech Industrial Park
Batu Tiga
40000 Shah Alam
Selangor Darul Ehsan
Malaysia
Fax & Tel: (603) 7363517

Printed by Vine Graphic Pte Ltd

ISBN 981 204 677 1

For my father and my mother

Contents

Preface

When I think of it now, I seem to have spent so much of my time, at least over the past few years, sitting in coffeeshops and stalls sipping oily-black coffee, observing the everyday passage of life out on the streets in front of me. The Malaysian *passagiero* of pork-sellers, Kayan matrons, *pak hajis*, schoolgirls and policemen, whether it be in Marudi, Sandakan, Batu Gajah or Balik Pulau, is as fascinating to me today as it always has been. Were it not for my present guise as a lawyer, I would still be sitting in those coffeeshops now, with an open notebook on my right, scribbling down as much as can possibly be written within the duration of one hot, sticky-sweet coffee. Almost invariably, I've ended up talking to the people sitting around me, listening to their stories. And it is these stories and impressions that have seeped into whatever I have subsequently written, colouring my views of my people, my country and my home just as the coffee, too, has left its inevitable browning stains on my notebooks.

I have never known a time when I wasn't either writing or preparing to write – reading, taking notes and conducting interviews. And, in this respect, I have been fortunate over the years in having the support of various newspapers and magazines, not to mention accommodating editors. Without the encouragement and positive criticism of editors such as Sheila Rahman (*New Straits Times*) and Walton Morais (*The Business Times Singapore*), I don't think I would have been able to cover the ground I have covered. Their constant reminders to me to be concise, accurate and, at times, more thoughtful have been an invaluable part of my years as a journalist. They, in turn, have had to wade their way through a torrent of words – much of which was more a reflection of a young man's untutored enthusiasms than any considered opinion. And it is out of this enthusiasm, my constant travelling and my reading that *Ceritalah*, my weekly column for *The Sun*, grew. I should add that the name

Ceritalah was coined by the poet-artist Latiff Mohidin, whose work has been a great inspiration to me.

I like to think of the columns as well as the longer pieces as being snapshots of a country and a people undergoing a series of momentous changes. I have to admit that having grown up in a very traditional family that placed a great deal of weight on the 'old ways', the subsequent dislocation has been, at times, almost overwhelming. I have long had many doubts about the speed with which we are moving and the way we are losing our own sense of history. The absence of self-knowledge in a grown man or woman is a personal tragedy. In the case of nations, it can lead to disaster. We must learn from our history and our respective cultures and apply those lessons in our everyday lives.

Having taken a position on the present condition of the political firmament, I can't say that my views necessarily reflect that of the majority. In fact, I've often been warned about the perils of my out-spokenness, about being too clear in a polity where opacity is the rule. However, Malaysia is undergoing a period of relative openness and my continued presence is a reflection of the latitude that is being afforded the press. The role of a writer in Malaysia is not an easy one. It is hard not to be truthful and whilst I've struggled for ways of avoiding offence, the strain has, in the end, reduced me to my present silence. I am a conservative in matters of economics and a liberal in matters of social policy, albeit a liberalism tempered by who and what we are, by our Asian identity, our respective faiths, philosophies and cultures. Malaysia is not an environment that is conducive to freedom of thought. At first I used to think the Government was responsible for this intellectual and creative poverty. I know better now. We are responsible for it – no one else. In this way, I hope that my relative candidness will encourage others to think and write. If we fail to record the swirling currents of life outside the coffeeshops, we may never be able to remember enough for our children and our children's children.

I would like to take this opportunity to thank the following for their kind permission in allowing me to republish the essays, articles and interviews in this book: Andy Ng, Philemon Soon, Alistair Tan, Kean Wong, Bob Ho and M. Menon of *The Sun*; Tuan Haji Zainun Ahmad, Datuk Kadir Jasin, Joanna Abishegam, Encik Ahmad Rejal Arbee, S. Jayasankaran, Steven K.C. Poh of Berita Publishing, the *New Straits Times Annual* and the *New Straits Times*; Faridah Stephens of *Men's Review*.

Travelling around the region, I would never have been able to view the various countries I visited with so much personal insight were it not for the fact of having generous friends such as Michael Vatikiotis and Rohana Mahmood who have been willing to share their experience. In South Africa, James Hersov, Mzi Khumalo, HE Mrs Maite Mohale, Mark and Susan Taylor have helped describe their infinitely complicated country. In Pakistan, Sayeda Matanat Mohsin and her family. In Thailand, Natayada Na Songkhla and Albert Paravi Wongchirachai. In Indonesia, Tara Sosrowardoyo (who also photographed the cover) and Nirwan Dewanto. In the Philippines, Karla Delgado and Christina Luz. In Japan, Joanna Pitman. In Singapore, Vidula Verma and her mother, Raj Verma. A writer depends on the generosity of others. Without them, I would be blind, deaf and dumb.

Once again I feel I should add that there is no doubt in my mind that the book you are holding now would not be in existence without the support and encouragement of the many editors I've mentioned, as well as Margaret Thomas and Jaime Ee of *The Business Times Singapore*, Marina Mahathir of *Sojourn* and Khalilah Mohd Talha of *Wings of Gold.* I have been very fortunate in having had the opportunity to work with a wide range of writers and editors. I must, however, single out Kean Wong for having the patience to edit all the *Ceritalah* columns. Without Kean's painstaking editing and thoughtful questions, I doubt I would have managed to achieve anything remotely readable. Added to them I must also mention a fellow writer Sheryll Stothard for her positive criticisms and my friend Valentine Willie for his support. Finally, I have to mention that the idea for the book was given to me by my good friend and ever-ready critic Saleha Mohd Ramly. On a personal note, I should add that the kindness and generosity of my patient 'foster-parents' Tuan Haji Ahmad Roose and Puan Hashimah bte Tun Abdul Aziz has given me the opportunity to reacquaint myself with my heritage, my culture and my faith.

The team at Times Editions – Shirley Hew, Shova Loh, Tan Jin Hock, Tuck Loong, Verena Tay and Christine Chong – has been dedicated, persistent and professional in all ways. Likewise, my partner Loong Caesar and the staff at Raslan Loong, especially Low Heng Hui, who first sifted his way through all the material so elegantly laid out on these pages.

Karim Raslan
Kuala Lumpur

Culture And Society

Our Cultures, Ourselves

The Sun: Ceritalah
27 May 1995

There are times when my interest (some might say unhealthy obsession) in what constitutes 'being' a Malay can get me into some pretty nasty arguments – ugly little exchanges that remind me of the laterite-red, scarred landscape around KL.

They're rarely very dignified and I seldom come away victorious. All too often I'm either tongue-tied and over-apologetic or aggressive and overbearing. Unfortunately, a happy medium tends to elude my grasp and generally, I'm left feeling both resentful and irritated.

Take last week, for example. I was in PJ, enjoying a seafood dinner with friends – chomping through Sri Lankan crabs at one of those garish restaurants where dragons seem to be jumping in and out of your retina. Sitting there, feeling (and perhaps looking) like a fat *angpow*, I attracted yet another barrage of criticism.

"Hey, Karim!" my fellow diner said, irritatedly, "how can you call yourself a Malay? Firstly, you hardly ever go to the mosque. Secondly, your Malay is so bad you sound like a Bangladeshi. Thirdly, you look like a bloody *Mat Salleh*."

Stunned by his outburst – we were only on the third course of a long dinner – I smiled weakly before replying. "Well, my father was Malay and I …"

"I've heard all that wimpy nonsense before. Don't bore me with it now. What I want to know is why you think you can speak for 'the Malays'? You, uh? It's a bloody joke. What next? Ramlah Ram for the UN?"

"Yeh," another friend piped up, "why are you so apologetic about the NEP? *Adoi*, it's pathetic. Sometimes I want to slap you around the face – all that Melayu angst."

Just then and perhaps luckily for me, the deep-fried pomfret covered in tom yam sauce arrived at the table, diverting everyone's attention. I say 'luckily' because to be honest, I realised that I had no real answers. In short, my inquisitors were right: how could I say, 'We Malays' and get away with it? How could I, a mere *Mat Salleh celup-writer*, possibly speak for a community of millions? A community so diverse that Anita Sarawak, Tok Guru Nik Aziz, Datuk Halim Saad, Sofia Jane Hisham and Datuk Nazri Aziz were just a few of its more well-known luminaries. However, the community – the *ummah* – was both diverse and monolithic. On the one hand, a Malay was expected to conform to certain set norms – many of which were quasi-feudal in their emphasis on loyalty, obedience and blind devotion to authority. Despite this, on the other hand, he was also expected to be a dynamic, cosmopolitan businessman, hunting down business opportunities in Yangon, Tashkent, Jo'burg and Santiago.

It was a thought that was to trouble me for many days. For example, I found myself wincing every time I caught sight of my own reflection in a shop-window or heard my own heavily accented Malay. Could I be a modern Malay and still be a Malay? Or had I, in fact, betrayed my roots, my *adat* and my faith by being so modern? It was enough to make my head spin painfully. After a while – to be quite honest – I began to feel rather paranoid. It was as if I felt somebody was watching me, checking to see how Malay I was being at any given time of day. I half-expected somebody to come after me and say 'Hey, you *jangan tipu lagi*. I know all about you – you're a fake'.

Finally, a week later, I began to sense an answer to my gathering paranoia. This time, another friend – an English-educated Chinese guy – was in the firing line. He had made the fatal miscalculation of launching into a lecture about 'We Malaysian Chinese ...' only to be shouted at from all sides. "You?" they all said, "You're a bloody banana: yellow on the outside and white on the inside!"

I smiled silently to myself as my friend parried the criticism – all too thankful that I wasn't in the firing line this time. However,

sitting there, slurping on slippery shark's fin soup, I suddenly realised that maybe I hadn't been so wrong in the first place. Could it be
that the two of us did have serious points to make about our respective communities and that we were fully justified in making them?
As far as I could see it, there were two issues at stake. Firstly it was
important to realise that 'being' Malay, Chinese or whatever was not
a categorical, strictly defined thing – not something that you could
tick off against some imaginary list: wears a sarong – yes; eats *sambal
belacan* – yes; eats durian – no. No? You can't be a Malay! Because
being a little (or a lot) different was actually good for the community
as a whole – diversity was strength and we had to be confident enough
to see that truth.

A cultural identity is not fixed. Contrary to what many people
may think, a Ming imperial ware vase is not a good metaphor for
Chinese culture. Chinese culture is continuously on the move – evolv-
ing slowly. It is shaped like the clay used in the Ming vase – both by
circumstance and environment from generation to generation. The
whole idea of being Chinese (much like the idea of being Malay)
differs radically from century to century and place to place. Historical and economic factors are constantly at work changing the immutable until Chinese culture, much like Malay culture, absorbs and
assimilates Western philosophy, Hindi movies, Disney's *Aladdin*, punk
rock, Sufism, Madonna, Chanel and Japanese cartoon books.

Secondly, I saw that my scribblings were important in one way
at least – if only because they presented you, the reader, with a fairly
honest opinion, an opinion that you were free to accept or reject.
And, since many of my opinions were often slightly at odds with the
mainstream, they, once again, provided an element of diversity – a
counterpoint to the general supine approach adopted by many other
writers.

A Moral Landslide

The Sun: Ceritalah
8 July 1995

Malaysia is not a land of physical disasters. There are no volcanic eruptions, typhoons or earthquakes. Whilst we are growing more accustomed to the presence of Bangladeshi workers, devastating floods on the Bangladeshi scale are, thankfully, unheard of. In short, our country has never been known for the kind of headlines that seem to plague nations like the Philippines, Zaire or India.

This, then, is part of the reason why the landslide on the Karak highway has caused such unease – or rather, why it should cause unease. I don't want to speculate about the reasons for the disaster – that is the business of the courts or an officially appointed body. Instead, I want to take the opportunity to stand back from the event and ask some questions. To my mind these questions should begin to tell us something about ourselves, our country and the value system that underpins our society.

However, before I begin, I should say that this is not an isolated event. It is a just one of a long succession of similar human-induced events that appear to have plagued the country in recent years. I say human-induced because we must ask ourselves a preliminary question. What were the people doing on that hillside in the first place? Should they have been there? I say this because we only have to look back to December 1993 and the Highland Towers collapse to be aware of the potential tragedies that can take place when man in his hubris tries to play God on earth. Perhaps we should face up to the fact that the land – our land – cannot be tamed in its entirety and that the quest for profit has to be quelled at a certain point.

Malaysians must stop and think. We must address these issues. For example, we must ask ourselves – is there such a thing as an acceptable level of risk where human life is concerned? If so, what is that level of risk? How do we balance the competing factors of human life, the environment and private capital? Should we, in fact, allow businessmen and politicians to run rampant – cutting corners and sacrificing standards? Is the free-market we extol, in fact, able to police itself?

I know, even before I begin, the arguments that the apologists for the present Malaysian 'value' system will propose. They will say that the country must progress and grow. And that growth can only come at the expense of the individual's rights. At times, they will say sadly, this may even mean growth at the expense of human life. This, they will say, is a penalty the country must pay if we are to move forward. This is the 'Asian value' argument adapted to Malaysia.

Well, I'm sorry but I will have to disagree. The 'Asian value' system does not mean a complete abandonment of the individual's rights and/or life. Neither does it mean a society where people can lie, cheat or be negligent, all in the name of profit and power. All societies, whether Asian or not, are possessed of judicial institutions that determine responsibility, liability and blame. Accountability and responsibility are part and parcel of the 'Asian value' system. They are not exclusively Western or modern. Confucius' *Analects*, the *Koran* and the *Bhagavad Gita* all talk about the righteous and responsible ruler. None of these three majestic texts advocates greed, favouritism or negligence.

The Government will have to respond to the public's demands for a thorough investigation. Tragedies such as this have to be dealt with in as transparent a manner as possible; responsibility must be ascertained, liability apportioned and the findings acted upon.

The tragedy then highlights the issues of accountability, planning and management – issues that will continue to haunt Malaysia (as well as all the other fast developing nations of the Asia Pacific) as it makes its push into the new millennia.

Economic growth over the past seven or so years has been exponential and it has increased the need to manage that growth. Encouraging and nurturing growth is one thing; controlling it and managing it is another. Growth and the prosperity it brings are, of course, of vital importance. But while there is a need to maintain growth, the country's leaders have to remember that they are mandated to be a whole lot more than prudent accountants. Dollars and cents are not the only yardstick by which Malaysians should judge their leaders' performance.

There will have to come a time when economic arguments and profit-making have to take second place to the community's broader needs such as health and safety. Forward planning and prudent management should have pre-empted such a catastrophe. Human lives should never be sacrificed in the quest for higher profit margins.

In the long run, the Malaysian elite – the cabal of businessmen and politicians that run our country – must realise that the strength and resilience of a society depends on its ability to enforce the law. Accountability is one way of showing that everyone is equal in the eyes of the law and that the Government is impartial. The cabal must not be allowed to get away unpunished if it is responsible. These deaths must not be in vain.

Value-Added Asians

The Sun: Ceritalah
26 November 1995

It's strange but true that much as there are fashions in popular music, clothes and art, there are also fashions in political and economic thought. Recently, I've been inundated with talk about Asian values and successes. Much as I'd love to jump on the self-congratulatory bandwagon, I can't help but be a contrarian because most of what I've been reading is sanctimonious, self-serving rubbish. Maybe I'm alone in this but I feel that we Malaysians are in danger of becoming smug and self-righteous in our views of what constitutes Asian values.

For a start, what are Asian values? Who is this elusive Asian? Is she the Thai prostitute squatting along the Chao Phraya river? Is he the Timorese farmer? Is he the Punan hunter? Secondly, what values do they share? I'm Asian but I don't think I have much in common with a South Korean factory worker or a stallholder in Tsimshatsui.

Quite frankly, most of this talk about Asian values is bogus and wrong-headed: people shouting their mouths off without defining their terms of reference. For example, I'd argue that Europeans and Americans also used to have a strong sense of family responsibility and duty, not to mention a belief in the importance of the community as a whole, over above the rights and freedoms of the individual. Whilst such values are no longer so potent or fashionable in Europe or the US, you only have to look at Victorian England or postwar Germany to realise their validity in the past.

What we must learn to do is treat the present talk of Asian values with a degree of healthy scepticism, winnowing out the relevant and useful from the rubbish. Principles of thrift, endeavour and family responsibility are not exclusively Asian – they are human values. Once we start thinking they are exclusively 'ours' we are in danger of considering ourselves as being morally better than non-Asians. Smug moral superiority is disgusting, whether the proponent is white, black, yellow or brown.

Next, I should add that the opinions of any writer or politician are obviously going to be shaped by the world around them. Writers and politicians have always been in search of the ideal utopian political and economic state. In the 1960s, Scandinavia (now in the throes of economic decline) seemed to offer the way ahead with its deceptively neat marriage of capitalism and socialism. To suggest the Scandinavian nations now as a blueprint would be to invite derision. As I said, fashions come and fashions go.

In the 1960s, for example, the talk was of the population explosion, underdevelopment, Third World poverty and the socialist remedies for the resolution of these problems. Scandinavians were in the forefront of these ideas. To read the Swede Gunnar Myrdal's *Asian Drama: An Inquiry into the Poverty of Nations* now is to experience an unpleasant but vaguely familiar time-warp.

Today's blueprint is Asian, and it's Asian because of the region's unbridled economic successes. Most of the Asian nations are economically free-market but politically inclined towards authoritarianism. I sum it up as a kind of 'work damn hard, live well but better not complain about debladiGubermen' (apologies to Kit Leee and Manglish) philosophy. Whilst the present utopia is Asian or at least an amalgam of characteristics present in the various Asian 'miracle' economies, it needs to be defined. Everyone refers to South Korea's automobile and semiconductor industries, Taiwan's family-run export-orientated successes, Singapore's stable society and China's phenomenal potential, forgetting as they do, that each of these nations is quite different: Chinese are not Koreans are not Vietnamese are not Thais are not Malaysians. In short, we Asians are a varied bunch.

What we've got to do now is realise that all this talk of Asian values needs more thought and serious consideration. Having accepted that the basis of the values is, in many ways, universal, we have to figure if there is anything that makes these values particularly Asian. Talking about them loosely as we are wont to do at the moment teaches us nothing. Furthermore, there are many so-called values that we might not want to preserve. Many Malays find our feudal background distasteful and backward. However, there may be others who worry about what we will be replacing our *adat* with, if we junk our supposedly Hinduistic culture.

Then we have to decide what Islamic values we are going to import into our society. Do we take on everything? There are a lot of differences of opinion and interpretations of the Syariah. What about our adoption of Chinese values? Which philosophers' works should we accept? Indian? And then what happens if the values are in opposition? Which one takes precedence?

I'm only playing devil's advocate because I feel the issue of Asian values *is* important. It is worth investing time and money in trying to formulate and synthesise our various cultural and religious systems into a Malaysian whole. Loose talk and ad hoc quotes from Chinese and Islamic scholars is a start. What is needed now is something solid and well-researched. It would be a shame if all this talk of 'Asian values' becomes another fashionable philosophy that disappears as suddenly as it first arrived.

Days Of Our Lives

The Sun: Ceritalah
24 June 1995

People often ask me questions about Malaysia and Malaysians – about who we are, where we're from and where we're going. I think it's because they realise that I'm 'hung-up' on this problem of identity, which I am. Having fielded so many of these questions over the years (am I a Malay Malaysian, a *Mat Salleh* Malaysian or an Anglo-Bumi Malaysian?), I've learnt that honesty and a degree of candidness is the key to the answer.

I can speak for myself and offer a view. Of course, anyone else is free to disagree. Because I'm not a politician I am happy enough with dissenting views. I answer by telling people stories and the first is about my birthday. I was born in August 1963. I like to think it's an auspicious month because I share the month, if not the exact date, with the nation – one of those little coincidences that bring a smile to your face. Unfortunately, being born at the same time as my country doesn't entitle me to anything very special.

No one's offered me a *Sasterawan*-ship, a pension or any pink share forms. In this respect, I'm quite unlike the magical characters in Salman Rushdie's novel *Midnight's Children* who came into the world just as Mother India was wrenched through her birth pangs and the bloodbath of partition (or was it parturition?). I'm just a simple, everyday Malaysian, though perhaps a little fatter and whiter than the norm, like the inside of large mangosteen. I eat *sambal belacan*, watch Hindi movies, get depressed when the KLSE drops below a 1000 points, play mahjong (badly), belch when the food is good and consider my kampung to be somewhere along Jalan Ampang, just after Ampang Park but before Hock Choon mini-market.

Having said that, I am, in my own way, a curious reflection of the whole. Because if we accept that Malaysia, the nation and its diverse people are the whole, then I, as a mix of Malay and English blood, am a combination of similar contrasts. I am just one of the many aspects of our nation, because Malaysia is the sum total of all these strange mixtures and all their stories.

I have memories of the past. Like everyone else, these memories colour my vision of both the present and the future, and because I am fitfully (it's been six years now) employed in writing a novel that draws its inspiration from the past, I, too, have been spending a great time mining both my own memories as well the memories of others. In doing so, one of the first things I've discovered is that my story is as much a part of the 'whole' nation's story as anyone else's.

There are times when the sharpness and pain of my memories – my father's death when I was a small child – obscure the lie of the land altogether. On the other hand, there are times when I feel everything is perfect – like when I'm eating the *chendol* from Penang Road Famous Chendol in Georgetown. I am not alone in this. I know a young woman, I'll call her Soraya, who lost both her father and her mother in a horrible boating accident. Understandably, the tragedy shaped her world unalterably and as a result, she became determined to succeed at all costs, helping her family along the way. Stories, then, are the essential flesh and blood of our lives: without them we would not be human.

A nation is much the same. It, too, has its memories, memories that are locked in the popular songs, jokes and stories that we tell one another. Some people call these memories, history. Whatever word you chose in the end, the function is the same. They are stories that remain dormant until they are retold, at which point they come alive again. Think of the word *hikayat*, which means amongst other things, the word 'story' in Malay. The word *hikayat* comes from Arabic: *hik-, hak-* which means to tell or recite and *ayat* which means verse or sentence. Passed from generation to generation in the stories our grandparents tell us, our *adat*, our customs, our novels and our films. And each of us is a part of the whole – Soraya's story is just as important as anyone else's.

However, some memories are worse than others. Some are fierce and frightening. They are the ones that are locked deep into the darkness that lies at the heart of the night. We wish that these could be forgotten but they cannot: they are an integral part of our making. National tragedies like the May 13 riots haunt us like an evil nightmare. Over the years (it's been 26 years now), the vividness of the memory decreases and we are able to confront the horror without wincing. That's age and maturity at work. So I, like my country, am growing fatter around the middle, a little wiser and hopefully, a whole lot more comfortable with who and what I am. Having said that, there are others who say that all countries are artificial and that nationalism is the nightmare of modern man.

The Ancient Art Of Reading Between The Lines

The Sun: Ceritalah

13 August 1994

We Malaysians are past masters of the ancient art of reading between the lines – we understand the importance of what's not said,
who's not said it and to whom he or she has not said it. Given the
complexities of the art and it is subtle and demanding, I'm hardly
surprised that Malaysians are reported to read only half a page of
newsprint every year. With that half a page they've read many more
pages of subtext. As one friend said to me soon after I returned home
after years abroad, "you learn to read the newspapers with a third
eye, an eye that scans for the subtext, an unwritten subtext."

I didn't believe him at the time but now I do. More than that,
nowadays, I'm actually quite adept at reading with my third eye –
though it does get a little strained from reading in the dark. In fact,
I use it so often nowadays that sometimes I think I should get glasses
for it as well. Glasses for a third eye is a peculiarly apt metaphor for
the society we live in.

But that's enough of the humour because the problem is very
real. It's as if we read the newspapers to be entertained and read
between the lines to be informed, observing the issues of the day as
they unfold step by step. The newspapers and editors are not entirely responsible for the problem. To blame them alone is to ignore
the root causes of the condition.

The recent cancellation of the vast Kedah theme park project
was a case in point. It came and went and in its wake, we were left to
ponder the reasons behind its arrival and departure. Sure, official
reasons were proffered. They always are. However, speculation has
taken over and as we all know, once speculation takes over it mutates
into a many-headed beast. Some people speculated that the project
was the victim of a rift between the Mentri Besar and the Federal

Government and others, a rift between the present and previous Finance Ministers. There are most likely a few coffeeshop politicos who think it is part of a British-inspired plot to blacken the good name of the country.

To be frank, we'll never know. And because we'll never know, the actual reasons are unimportant. The rumour mill, that many-headed beast I was talking about, has started up and, having started up, it has taken on a life all of its own. The authorities can deny the rumours as much as they want, as often as they want. No one will believe them. This, then, is the problem with the third eye: it distorts our perception of the world.

How does it distort our perceptions? Well, it makes us consider everything in terms of personality and clique. Now, the world of politics is, to a large extent, about personality: we vote for particular individuals because of how they appear in person. What the third eye does is magnify this aspect of the political process until it overwhelms all else. We tend not to think in terms of principles because we are always looking for personal motives: the people who will benefit from any particular transaction and by how much they will benefit.

So what is the solution for this approach? How can we overcome this myopia? Because three eyes can leave you just as short-sighted as two. The key lies in the transparency of Government and in the need for greater accountability. Decisions have to be taken in the open and the reasons for any particular course of action aired and debated upon. As our public life becomes more transparent and people become accountable for the decisions they have taken, the need for all this confusing speculation will begin to drift away into inconsequence.

The Art Of Writing Between The Lines

The Sun: Ceritalah
20 August 1994

Last week, I wrote about the Malaysian reader's third eye – the eye
that scans the newspapers for what's hinted at but never actually
written in the text. This week, I thought I'd write about the art (and
the pitfalls) of writing between the lines – yes, you heard me right,
writing between the lines – the art of writing for the reader who is
practised in the art of reading between the lines (phew!). I think
what I have to say should help explain why the Malaysian papers are
as boring as they are (*The Sun* excepted, of course).

Firstly, the obvious point: writing between the lines is a precari-
ous business. If the journalist is not too careful, he or she will end up
falling off the lines altogether. And once he's fallen off, chances are
he'll never get back up again. The whole business then requires a
degree of dexterity that can leave his reputation in tatters if he gets it
wrong. But before you, the reader, scratch your head in confusion,
let me explain.

The best way to illustrate what I have to say is to use the example of a gymnast working out on the parallel bars. Think of the bars
as the 'lines' and the gymnast as the 'writer', and you'll understand
what I mean. The gymnast on the parallel bars doesn't actually rest
on the bars for any length of time. Instead, he throws himself all
over them; above them, below them and between them – grabbing
them every now and then for balance. A momentary loss of concentration or control and he's a goner.

Well, the journalist is in much the same position. He or she can
allude to certain things – money politics, State and Federal tensions,
corruption – without being able to point the finger at anybody. Always contorting himself by throwing his body all over the place. As a
result, he's faced with all these issues and problems that appear to

have no cause (some of us call them the 'causeless issues') because no one person or persons is responsible for anything.

Professionally, this can be very dissatisfying. Good journalists want to get to the root of a story. They want explanations; explanations they know they'll never get. So they keep on throwing themselves around, in the hope that no one notices they're not really doing anything very special or productive. This wouldn't matter were it not for the fact that a journalist is expected to voice the concern of the people he or she is writing for. I, for example, am writing for *The Sun* reader. In many ways, I'm also hoping to articulate what you, as non-writers (because you're too busy in the main), would like to say but haven't got the time to say.

If I go off on a hopeless tangent and write about the rights of the North American Indian or the gay badger (apparently they exist), you're not going to be too interested. No one will read my column, the editors will lose interest and I will be terminated forthwith. Just like that. You want to read about Malaysia because you are a Malaysian. However, being a Malaysian doesn't mean that you want to read all that frothy nonsense about how well we're doing.

You know that. You want to read about the problems in society and business, on how they can be resolved. However, writing about such things won't make me too popular with the powers-that-be. Before you know it, everyone will be reading my column, the editors will get edgy and I will be terminated forthwith. Just like that. Hey, hang on! Doesn't that sound rather what like what would happen if no one read my column? Ah ha! Now you're getting it … Basically, you're damned if you're boring and damned if you're not. Which leaves the half-world between the 'lines' as your only refuge.

As you can see, a journalist treads an awkward path. He's beholden to his masters and – if he's honest with himself – rather intimidated by their power. On the other hand, he realises that if he's to become a writer of any stature, he has to start writing about the things that his masters (political or otherwise) don't want to have written about. Yes, if I was writing for the powers-that-be, regurgitating the nonsense that I'm force-fed with everyday, I'll soon discover that no one wants to listen to me.

A writer's stock-in-trade isn't just his ability to write, it's also his *amanah*, or truthfulness. And if I compromise this, I'll find that readers will become less and less inclined to believe what I have to say. Serving his political masters hand and foot can be very good for his career but it makes a mockery of his profession. Once his integrity is sullied, once people know he is a toady, no one is ever going to believe him again. We all know who the toadies are – I don't have to tell you.

For my part, I'll continue to write between the lines until the time comes when I can start writing on the lines. I'll be performing all the feats of an acrobat, hanging onto my *amanah* for all its worth. I hope I don't slip.

Bound By Duty

The Sun: Ceritalah
10 December 1994

I have to confess that the moment I read about the Amanah Saham Bumiputra's (ASB) returns for 1994, I dashed off to calculate how much money was due to me.

However, as I was counting my returns, I was suddenly struck by the thought that my entitlement to the ASB and its remarkable rate of return was something that I took for granted, a right I enjoyed without a commensurate responsibility or duty. Was I different from an European receiving unemployment benefits? If so, how?

The question of rights and duties troubled me, and it was lucky that I happened to be reading a book called *The Principle of Duty* by British academic David Selbourne. Briefly, the book seems to argue that (in the West, at least) the issue of individual rights had reached such a fever pitch that whole societies were in danger of disintegrating under the conflicting demands of various pressure groups.

Selbourne argues that the purpose of a state is not to propel the rights and needs of the individual – this can bring about anarchy. The state must be concerned with the needs of the community as a whole, and the duties owed to the community by the individual. A classic example of this conflict would seem to be the court case brought against the British government by the World Development Movement (WDM), which sought to invalidate the Pergau dam project.

The project was undertaken by the British for a number of political and economic reasons, not least of which was the need to prove their *bona fides* to the Malaysian government in order to rebuild a potentially profitable commercial relationship. However, WDM's victory was a triumph of the individual's interests over the community's.

Now this premise may sound familiar to anyone following the whole business of 'Asian values'. In both cases, we're concerned with a system of values that sees the well-being and stability of the community and civic order over and above the rights of the individual. Let me explain: this means the prosperity and security of Malaysia is more important than my right to say, clean air or a free press. The factories and cars that spew out pollution are vital to our economic well-being, just as the controlled press is necessary for political stability. In short, my rights are secondary in this equation.

Of course, Western conditions differ from our own. Over there, the pursuit of individual rights has reached the point where very few people are concerned about the health and well-being of the civic order as a whole. Selbourne argues that people are reduced to the level of "moral strangers snarling across a disintegrating void", a loose set of individuals arguing over the rights due to them – forgetting, of course, that without a commensurate set of duties and responsibilities, there can be no functioning community.

Moreover, he argues that the rhetoric of socialism has been grafted on to the concept of rights to create a sub-group of economic rights. By this he means that people are convinced that they possess an economic right to well-being, comfort and prosperity, things the state was bound to provide, whether or not they bothered working and whether or not they deserved it.

It was this point that worried me about the ASB. Did people like me see ASB as 'a gravy train', a set of inalienable rights for which we had to do nothing in order to receive it?

Were we Malaysians in danger of falling into a similar situation?

So what are these duties that Selbourne feels need to be preserved and enhanced? For a start, the well-being of the community is essential. Therefore, it is our duty to keep the community stable. How do we achieve this? Simple, at least according to Selbourne: we must educate our children about civic responsibility, buttress up the family unit (thus preventing the occurrence of *boh sia*, etc), and stress the paramount importance of participation in the society at large because the community's needs are always more important than the individual's. Having read of these duties, I wondered whether I had carried out all my responsibilities.

I know these arguments might sound familiar to any Malaysian, but what troubled me was the way my entitlement to the ASB could be categorised as an economic right and the fact that the idea of economic rights was in opposition to the whole ethos of 'Asian values'. Of course, I understand the importance of political circumstance and the need to redress age-old economic and social grievances. Nonetheless, there can be no doubt that there is a disturbing contradiction here. The problem with economic rights is that they can breed complacency and greed – unemployment benefit in the West is a case in point.

Driving around the middle-class ghettoes of Taman Tun, Subang Jaya and Melawati, I wondered whether we weren't in danger of creating a class of people who would be unable to live without such entitlements? In a fiercely competitive world, Malaysians should rethink the whole question of economic rights. Could these rights be the thin end of the wedge? The wedge that brings with it the disintegrating societies of the West?

Faith Healing

The Sun: Ceritalah
4 February 1995

I imagine many people would secretly agree with me when I confess that I've never found either religion or philosophy to be subjects of much interest. The bigotry of the first and the pedantry of the second has long been an anathema to me, not to mention the smug, self-righteous tone of those who profess to be religious. Besides that, there has always been the underlying sense that religion and philosophy are somehow no longer relevant and that in a world of ever-spiralling scientific achievements, the role of God – any God – has become redundant.

However, I've recently had to change my views. I haven't become a religious zealot overnight, don't worry. Far from it. Over the past few weeks, however, I've been busy reading and re-reading a whole host of holy books from the *Koran*, the *Bhagavad Gita* and the *Hadiths* to the *Analects* and the *Dhammapada*. Eclectic and to my surprise, enlightening as well. What I had once thought of (in my ignorance) as being irrelevant to my yuppie KL life, contained a great deal which proved to be far more pertinent and resonant than I had ever thought possible.

I should say that I wasn't in search of enlightenment or meaning when I first started out on my reading. I was looking for material related to the issue of 'Asian values'. Basically, I suddenly realised that I lived in Asia. Now, I know that this may sound stupid but as a Western-educated Malay, I was more familiar with likes of Aristotle and Plato than I ever was with my own philosophical and religious traditions. And when I say my own traditions, what did I mean?

Well, Malaysia is one of the few countries in the world where all the great Asian faiths and philosophies have come into contact with one another. As such, these faiths and philosophies – Hinduism,

Confucianism, Islam and the like, belong to us as much as they do to India, China or Arabia. I now see that it is for us to appropriate the positive attributes of the cultures, faiths and philosophies that constitute our nation. And this was precisely what I was up to when I was reading all these holy books.

For a start, all philosophies of life and religions are concerned with the problem of life and living: a combination of "why the hell are we here?" and "what are we going to do about it now?" As such, they contain two basic themes: a reason for living (the Heavens hereafter or the termination of the cycle of rebirth are two examples) and the way in which we should go about the 'living'. Both Confucius and Lao Tzu, for example, talk of the 'Way' or 'Tao' – the means by which a gentleman achieves a life of truth, virtue and benevolence.

Contrary to my expectations, all the holy books advocated an active engagement in life. Somehow I'd expected them to preach withdrawal and retreat – but they didn't. Each seemed to call on the believer to be involved *in* society, to be an active participant in life, to live fully and share in that living. In the *Bhagavad Gita*, for example, a nervous warrior, Prince Arjuna, is told by Lord Krishna that enlightenment is not a question of withdrawing from the world. And Lord Krishna says so powerfully, in a manner that suggests the coming battle on the plains of Kurukshetra as a metaphor for life in general:

> *"Therefore rise up, Arjuna, resolved to fight! Having made yourself alike in pain and pleasure, profit and loss, victory and defeat, engage in this great battle and you will be freed from sin."*

In the same way, Confucius and Mencius call on their readers to take an active, thoughtful and virtuous role in all they undertake. In Mencius' famous exposition of 'human-heartedness' (*jen*) that revolves around the possibility of a child falling down a well, man's sensitivity, his alarm and distress, is comparable with "a fire that begins to burn or a spring which has begun to find vent" – a force for good that can be developed so that "they (men) will protect all within the four seas."

I also a found a wonderful *hadith* that called on everyone to see themselves as a ruler, entrusted with the care of those under him or her: rulers of their subjects, husbands of their wives, mothers of their children and so on, a seamless web of responsibilities and duties that bound the real world into one.

So, on the one hand, I discovered the continuing relevance and deep resonance of religion and faith, seeing that religion in its pure unadulterated form at least, extolled knowledge, beauty and virtue. On the other hand, I saw the outlines of an Asian value or principle based on an amalgam of all these holy books – the principle of duty. Briefly, I saw that men and women had a duty to be involved in society, to partake in life rather than to withdraw unto themselves. I should conclude by quoting Confucius who said, "Simply by being a good son and friendly to his brothers, a man can exert an influence upon government."

Open Season

The Sun: Ceritalah

1 July 1995

The Malaysian Open House season (dubbed the Malaysian Open by insiders) is looming on the horizon. The caterers are limbering up, the suppliers stocking up, the players in training and my stomach quaking at the thought. Beginning with Deepavali in November and then swiftly followed by Christmas, New Year, Chinese New Year and Hari Raya all in quick succession, culminating in the triennial Umno General Assembly, the Malaysian Open of '95–'96 will be one of the toughest on record.

Having lived through the last season (and that was without the added Umno complication), I'm warning all serious competitors to start planning their line of attack now because this is serious. This is war.

Tora! Tora! Or how I survived the Malaysian Open – 157 and a half (I crashed the half) open houses – and lived to tell the tale. The Malaysian Open requires patience, stamina and an iron-plated stomach. The seeded players are younger, tougher and meaner this year. International exposure has given them an edge. The added complication of the Umno General Assembly means this year's Open will be a hotly contested one.

But first of all, a few basic principles: the number of fans and air-cons installed in a house is in inverse proportion to the heat and the humidity; ergo, the hotter it is, the less fans there are; secondly, the only bits of chicken left in the *lauk* are the bottom and the neck – the host will blame the caterer but we know he's economised on the chicken; thirdly, refusing *angpows* when you're a 32-year-old and unmarried is uncool; fourthly, being 32 and unmarried is even more uncool; fifthly, you'll never remember your host's wife's name; finally, if that's the case, you're most likely in the wrong house.

But who cares – welcome to the Malaysian Open, where the object is to notch up as many house visits without collapsing under the pressure. The Open can also teach you a few things about logistics. It's rumoured that freight-forwarders, Umno division heads and MAS Kargo staff have been assigned to the Open to build up their confidence and stamina. For example, you'll soon learn that you can't cram more than 10 sticks of *satay*, *rendang*, *ayam kuzi*, mutton curry, roast lamb, *nasi briyani* and *roti jala* on your plate without dropping it on your host's mother's favourite Italian silk *baju* or the sofa that's just been bought from Fella.

The rule of thumb is eat as little as possible. Finally, never ever own up to dropping food on the furniture – especially if it's from Janine's. Always blame the kids.

The Open is riddled with obstacles. The scruffy little man you asked to park your car – you mistook him for a valet – is, in fact, the richest, best-informed stockbroker in town; the man who wanders around the house and acts as if he owns the place, barking orders at the servants and the caterers, is invariably a gate-crasher.

Avoid cute little babies. They tend to vomit on your lap – something their mothers will find 'adorable'. Keep away from smug relatives. They will insist on *puasa enam* whilst asking you in front of all assembled how many days you managed to fast. The rose syrup will be so sweet it'll rot your teeth as you drink it. And roast lamb cannot be eaten with a spoon and fork.

Of course, there are moments to treasure, moments of rare poetic justice. That big-mouthed, cigar-toting businessman who advised you to buy Aokam at RM30 (because it'll go to RM50) is now driving a 10-year-old Nissan Sunny. Then there are plump *mak datins* and *tai-tais* who tell you about their love for literature, Jeffrey Archer and John Grisham – "wasn't Michael Douglas good in the book?"

I enjoy watching once-powerful politicians melting into the corners of the living room when the new 'rising' men and women (the seeded players) arrive to take centre stage. If you're lucky, you can see them grovelling: always enjoyable. Then there are pasty-faced, dim-witted diplomats who smile and shake hands with the barman because they think he's a senior civil servant.

Of course, dressing correctly is crucial. Avoid all man-made fibres unless you're going to a Deepavali open house, in which case, the rule is simple: the brighter, the better. Another tip for Deepavali open houses is to say *"Guinness-Stout-Ungehlehkeh-naladah"* or "Guinness Stout is good for you" in Tamil. This will bring the house down.

But back to the clothing. Avoid batik shirts that make you look like a Dulux paint sample, and wear shirts that are at least two sizes too large. Otherwise, the silk has a tendency to cling to your belly. Wear lots of aftershave at all times to save your host and hostess from being asphyxiated by your BO.

The '95–'96 Open will see the 'arrival' of a whole new generation of players: men and women who will have battled their way through at least a decade of Opens. After having spent the first few years sitting under the car porch and battling with the crowds for that last stick of *satay*, they will have graduated to the premier league. Now, they will be sitting in the 'air-conded' living room, holding court. Adept players in the Open rise fast. If I were you, I'd get into training now.

Pleasing Himself First

The Sun: Ceritalah

22 October 1994

I once wrote that Salleh ben Joned was 'a star'. At the time, it was half in jest. Now I'm sure of it. What makes me so sure? I've just read his collection of essays published by SKOOB Pacifica called *As I Please*. Reading these essays, most of which were originally published in the *New Straits Times* over the past few years, has reminded me of the enormous pleasure I received at their first reading.

There's no doubt in my mind that Salleh is one of the most important writers in Malaysia at the moment. He stands above all the others for three reasons: firstly, he has a written style that is superb; secondly, his arguments are deft and rapier-sharp; thirdly and finally, he is willing to challenge all accepted norms. In short, the man has balls.

And, in a country like Malaysia where most academics and writers are as supine and lacklustre as neutered lapdogs, his sheer exuberance and balls-iness is like an injection of steroids to the brain. Part of the reason I like his work so much is because he writes (literally) with balls.

He revels in the ribald and the licentious. His reading of Malay *pantuns* is infused with the passion and eroticism that most Malaysian literary critics would prefer to overlook. And, like any good poet, he adores language, throwing in puns and jokes by the dozen. In an essay, the *Salacious Pleasures of Pantuns* (note the pun on 'Salleh' and 'salacious'), he dwells on 'tits tilting against the *baju*'. In another essay, critics come in for a deserved bashing. And he is at pains to explain the linguistic roots of the word in Malay, saying 'Critic – *kritikus – tikus*' (mouse). I should add that Salleh's well-publicised spat with the Malay literary community has only made me more keen to read their works. Whether or not I like or admire them is my decision. Nonetheless, he has sparked off my interest and hopefully yours, too.

Having said that, Salleh is not frivolous. He sees the humour and passion of Malay life and culture as something we are in danger of losing. He tries to bridge the growing chasm by sweeping, in one flourish of the pen, from the world of real men and women (and not priggish, sermonising *lebais*) to subjects of high seriousness such as Islam, the Malay identity and the Malay language. I feel that in acknowledging the earthy roots of the Malay world, his writing possesses a degree of authenticity that many others lack. He is a breath of fresh air whose literary antecedents are men like the Indonesian poet Chairil Anwar, whose poem *Aku* is a paean to individuality and the bohemian life:

> *Aku ini binatang jalang*
> *Dari kumpulannya terbuang ...*

> *I am a wild beast*
> *Driven from the herd ...*

However, my respect for Salleh rests to a large extent on his willingness to tackle the rarely discussed issues of race, religion and identity. He is bold and firm in his views. In all cases he tries, as he says in his own words, "to see through and beyond the inherited blinkers of race and religion," acknowledging that in doing so, he is danger of being considered a traitor to his race, "loyalty to truth and beauty, justice and freedom can be considered a betrayal." In his essay *The (Malay) Malaysian Writer's Dilemma*, he examines the effect of "convenient pieties about ethnic survival and dominance" on the Malay writer.

His views on Kassim Ahmad's book on the *Hadiths* is an important instance of dialogue in Islamic theology. It is thought-provoking and rests on some (I imagine) fairly solid research and reading. There is one line, in particular, of the *Koran* that he refers to time and again – *La ikraha fi'd'di'*, meaning there is no compulsion in religion (*al Baqarah*, verse 256). And it is a line that is well worth remembering, especially if one believes in the importance of *ijtihad*, or individual judgment, vis-à-vis Islam as opposed to *taqlid*, or imitation or blind acceptance of authority.

Salleh's advocacy of the use of English is cogent and powerful. He sees the language as being racially neutral and argues that the language has been appropriated by Malaysians to such an extent that it now belongs to us. "It is *our* English," he writes, "along with BM it expresses our 'soul' with all its contradictions and confusions as much as our social and material needs." It is a hopeful argument. However, he is being ingenuous because English has become a language of the elite, a passport to a world of greater opportunity and position.

Whatever Salleh's views on race, religion and language they are always entertaining and well-argued. A consummate essayist, his brand of tolerance is infectious. I only hope that the smug, bigoted so-called intellectuals will catch the bug. I'll leave you with one observation. According to Salleh, in the Philippine language of Tagalog, the word 'Malaya' means freedom or consciousness. Trust Salleh …

The Welcome Mat

The Sun: Ceritalah
28 January 1995

My seafood lunch is served by charming English-speaking Burmese, my car petrol tank refilled by Bangladeshis, the roads and buildings made by Indonesians, the adverts shot and produced by Australians and my friends' houses cleaned by Filipinos and their children taken care of by Thais. Where am I living? Where else but Kuala Lumpur, Asia's most alluring 'Pot of Gold', the nirvana of émigrés from Pakistan through to mainland China.

Now, all Malaysians have different views on the issue of immigration and the many millions of foreigners currently living in Malaysia. I know a good many who'd be quite happy machine-gunning the Indonesians and Filipinos as they land on the beaches of Johor and Sabah respectively. Others, whilst not so extreme in their views, would have all the foreigners – this includes the Australian and British economic refugees as well – corralled and tightly regulated.

I am afraid I have to disagree with both schools of thought. I'm all for throwing open our doors as widely as possible – allowing in as many people as want to come. Why am I so liberal in my views? The answer is simple. Malaysia is nation that is built on the sweat, determination and ingenuity of its immigrants. Indirectly this issue can also teach us something very important about ourselves.

I should add that when I use the word 'immigrant', I don't just mean those of us who came from China and India. Because, by using the word 'immigrants', I am also referring to the many Malaysian Malays who came from Sumatra, Java and Sulawesi, the ones who bequeathed us the *Tuhfat al-Nafis* with its descriptions of the Bugis warriors who were to lay the foundations for many prominent Royal Houses in Malaysia today.

Whatever anyone may say about the word immigrant and its Malay equivalent *'pendatang'*, I should add that my father, too, was descended from Bugis seamen who settled in Kota Lama, Perak in the 1800s – quite sometime after the resplendent Nonya families of Malacca such as Tan Siew Sin's forebears, for example. Whilst my family can at least claim to have lived in what is now Malaysia for several generations, I know many prominent Malays whose Achehnese, Javanese or Mendeling ancestry is far, far more recent.

So, what is my point? Malaysia is a country where nationality is as much a state of mind as it is an accident of birth or a set period of residency. We've all of us pitched up here over the years and since 1963, we've been Malaysians. This doesn't mean we've lost touch with our mother cultures – the Chinese are culturally Chinese and the Indians, Indian but they are as fiercely proud of being Malaysian as I am.

But as I said earlier, being Malaysian is as much a state of mind as anything else. I feel that there are two central principles to our public life. I may well be wrong, perhaps too simplistic and I'd be very happy to be corrected on this point. Nonetheless, it is fairly important for us to figure out who and what we are – to probe our national psyche so that in times of future strife, we're prepared to tackle the problems that may descend.

Whatever it is, let me get back to my principles: firstly, you can't really be a true consensus-seeking Malaysian if you insist on ramming the Syariah law or any other culturally and religiously exclusive set of laws down the throats of all other Malaysians. Why? Because this country is about allowing people – within limits, of course – to chose how they wish to lead their lives as long as essentially the vitality and good health of the community is not jeopardised.

Secondly, you can't be a true Malaysian if you don't believe in the essential ability of every man and woman to better themselves because Malaysia, unlike so many other countries, does not condemn those born in poverty to poverty and ignorance for life. I see this as an extension of Confucius' saying that the ultimate purpose of government is the welfare (*min*) of the common people – in short, allowing the people to prosper by providing an administration that is fair and wise.

Unsurprisingly, these two basic principles are extremely attractive to many people living in neighbouring countries. And when many of them manage to make the desperate journey here, some in fragile *kumpits* and *prahus*, all they want to do is live and work as hard as the rest of us. In short, these people are here because they believe in what Malaysia has to offer, because they – often without realising it – subscribe to the two central principles of our public life. So, I say let them all come, relax the immigration regulations, allow them to acquire nationality and turn them all (Australians and British included) into true blue Malaysians.

Our Changing Natures

The Sun: Ceritalah
18 March 1995

There are certain subjects that I, as a writer and a fiercely proud Malaysian, have tended to shy away from, if only because too close an analysis of them might threaten my precious ideals about my country. The subject of race has, for so long, been so sensitive that all too often writers such as myself have chosen to ignore it. It's never been an issue I have enjoyed writing about. However, it is unavoidable in any serious analysis of who and what we are. Because of this, I've always been wary of what I might uncover in my writings. So, rather like a man at a public execution, I have stood near the gallows with my eyes closed whilst listening to what's been going on, gritting my teeth and shaking my head all the while: feeble but true. Most writers, myself included, are enormous cowards.

However, at a recent conference in South Africa where I'd been invited to talk about the Malaysian 'success' story along with Michael Yeoh of ASLI, I was struck not by the iniquities and injustices of the racial paradigm in Malaysia but by the views of my fellow speakers from South Africa, the US and the Middle East. To be quite frank, it was as if Michael and I had landed on Mars. They spoke a gobbledygook called 'Politically Correct Language', wherein all blacks were dispossessed, disadvantaged, deserving and noble. Of course, none of them were lazy, stupid or ignorant.

For a start, nobody was very interested in what we had to say – which was strange because we actually came from one of the very few successful multiracial nations in the world. In the case of the others, especially the pair from the Middle East, it was as if an economist from Mexico had been invited to talk about currency stability and a North Korean about diplomacy. I did suggest that the Middle East might not be the best place to learn about racial harmony but nobody seemed too concerned. Anyhow, the conference organisers knew better because the audience for the session on the American experience, for example, filled a substantial hall three times the size of the one slated for the talk on Malaysia – proof, if proof was need, that people enjoy listening to bad news.

However, I should add that the reason for the high attendance was most probably because the conference organisers had, in their infinite wisdom, invited the academic Charles Murray, author of the controversial *The Bell Curve: Intelligence and Class Structure in American Life* to talk about racial problems in the US.

Listening to him speak – he was an urbane and sophisticated man – I suddenly realised that his premise, his view of race, seemed to be based on genetics. This sent the Malaysian Chinese lady tycoon next to me into a fit of outraged apoplexy. I tried to remain calm but unless I was completely mistaken, which was quite possible because I was only a lowly Malaysian, Murray seemed to be propagating a view of race that stressed the characteristics of birth and heredity over environment and education. Shocked by his views, I slumped in my seat whilst my neighbour fumed.

"*Mat Sallehs!*" she said, "What do they know?"

His black counterpart Cornell West, an academic from Harvard, seemed no better. He argued that generations of deprivation and oppression meant that the Afro-Americans (what was wrong with the term 'Black', I wondered?) deserved better treatment from the whites and the US Government. It was all guilt-based: you mistreated us then, now you must pay. At this point, my exasperated countrywoman burst out irritatedly.

"*Aiyah!* What about thrift and education-lah."

Well, I was furious too, but more because neither man really seemed to see that racial stereotypes could be changed, albeit over time. Both seemed to be positing a world in which black men remained mired in the underclass because they had smaller brains and bigger dicks. In my anger I saw, perhaps for the first time, that the

Malaysian approach to the idea of race was a great deal more positive and dynamic. However, in the sea of hands, my own questions and those of my neighbour, a Chinese version of Rafidah Aziz, were lost

Walking out of the hall, talking to my neighbour – though I should add that in the tradition of her namesake, she talked at me more than the other way around – I saw that race was a set of cultural attributes that could be altered and changed over the years. For example, Syed Hussain Alatas' treatise *The Myth of the Lazy Native* had almost become a historical curiosity because of changing circumstances and 'mindsets' in the Malay community.

Both of us agreed (I nodded; she did the talking): me the Malay, and she the Chinese lady tycoon, that no one had said the obvious, which was that education, thrift, family-mindedness, filial piety and hard-work made a vast difference in the equation. No one said that the disadvantaged people had to work to change themselves. No one said that lazy, feudalistic, fatalistic, ignorant, spendthrift people do not deserve any better. No one talked about education, moral or cultural values. No one at all. Or rather, no one until the Malaysians spoke up.

A Salutary Lesson

The Sun: Ceritalah
3 December 1994

Flying across the South China Sea one day, between Johor Bahru and Kota Kinabalu, I found myself sitting next to a short, slightly wizened 50-year-old, songkok-wearing Malay man. We observed one another surreptitiously for the first half of the journey. He glanced over the top of his reading glasses at the pile of newspapers I was ploughing through (journalists read newspapers like *mak datins* shop – voraciously) and I watched him making notes on a large pad of paper.

He was dark-skinned and his hands looked roughened. I wondered where he was from, guessing that he was most likely a schoolteacher returning from some kind of teaching seminar in the peninsula. Our mutual curiosity got the better of us and before long we were deep in conversation.

As I had guessed, he was from Kota Belud and he was a schoolteacher. But, to my surprise, he wasn't a Sabahan as I had expected. He was a Johorean and his nicely clipped Bahasa reaffirmed his Riau roots. However, he had spent well over 20 years in Sabah, so there was that lovely lilt to his Malay and the occasional 'bah' instead of 'lah'.

Talking to schoolteachers is something I've always enjoyed, and Mustapha Mohammad (not his real name) was no exception. There's a clarity and single-mindedness in the best of teachers; they talk directly and warmly, pausing every few minutes to check whether or not you have followed what they have to say. As we talked, I was reminded of the most inspiring teacher I'd ever had. Contrary to what you might expect, he was a Malay primary schoolteacher, but let me explain a little more first.

When I first came back home after some 15 years abroad, I was lucky enough to be introduced to a retired Malay language teacher called Cik Gu Mohamed Amin – Mohamed Amin the Teacher. Teaching me three times a week, he helped me through my Malay language test for the Bar. In retrospect, I have to admit that I've never had such a brilliant teacher: he was impassioned, tolerant, honest and devout, encapsulating a host of qualities that one finds all too rarely in life.

Cik Gu was a product of the vastly underrated Tanjung Malim Teachers Training College. Most important of all, however, was the fact that he was still enthused with the idea of teaching as a calling and this enthusiasm was contagious. He opened up for me the world of Malay literature and culture, a world that I had only half-known. It made me realise the duality of my inheritance. It's at this point that I should add that when I was a small boy, *Cik Gu* was an important title. You sat up properly if you were introduced to a *Cik Gu* and listened to what they had to say. If you didn't agree, you never argued back: they were older and therefore wiser.

In more modern parlance, you gave them the benefit of the doubt. I remember that when we visited my father's kampung in Kuala Kangsar, we would be introduced to 'Cik Gu so-and-so' and be expected to treat the man (he was normally grey-haired and rather wizened) with extreme deference. In fact, my father was so attached to his *Cik Gu's* that they became surrogate uncles – men he would turn to for advice or peace of mind.

I may be old-fashioned but to my mind, the way we treat our educators, teachers and headmasters is a reflection of how we value education in the broader sense. Everyone grovels when a KLSE-listed CEO or an Umno Division Chief walks in: the embodiments of money and power respectively.

Nowadays, however, no one is too concerned about a teacher, the embodiment of education and knowledge. In short, it's nothing very important in the modern-day context. What this reveals is a worrying paradox at the heart of the Malaysian approach to education – a paradox that is endangering the profession.

If you meet a *Cik Gu* nowadays, they'll be rather embarrassed about their job, their miserable pay and their relative unimportance in present-day society. They'll cringe at being called *Cik Gu*, for a start. Teachers – who cares ?

Well, I'm afraid we should care. We Malaysians have a tendency to be rather big-headed about our achievements and myopic about our failings. We can reel off a list of firsts – the first car, the first flights to Latin America, the tallest buildings. But we tend to forget, for example, that our literacy levels are appalling. With illiteracy running at 22% of the population, we are lagging behind far poorer countries like Sri Lanka and Indonesia.

Education is all very well – everyone wants it, or rather the paper qualifications that you nail up on your wall along with your graduation photograph. But no one appears to be too concerned about the people entrusted with the task. All I hope is that there are men and women like Cik Gu Mohamed Amin and his Sabahan colleague teaching the present generation of schoolchildren because their contribution to society is woefully neglected.

Sadly, this is where we reveal our fatal weakness. Because the education that we receive can only be as good as the people entrusted with that responsibility. Treating them like dirt will help no one.

Test-Tube Baby

The Sun: Ceritalah
14 January 1995

One morning, instead of clambering out of bed and getting off to work, I accidentally pressed the television remote control, flicking on the TV in my bedroom. Within seconds, I was hooked, forgetting all my appointments, my work, everything. I had been zapped into an alternative reality – let's call it celluloid reality – a world or rather, a plane of existence where everything comes to an abrupt halt every 20 minutes or so. That's right. Phut! And we're out of celluloid reality into advertising reality (another plane of existence where only two voices – Yasmin Yusoff's and Harith Iskander's prevail). In advertising reality, we are fortunate enough to receive a few choice images and words of wisdom from the sponsors: a kind of subtle "BUY ME! BUY ME!" sales pitch.

But back to celluloid reality. Celluloid reality is a world where everything is possible: a world where insinuating black women multimillionaires thrust microphones into the faces of wayward and impoverished boyfriends as studio audiences cheer her on; a world where talented Malay singers practise arpeggios beside grand pianos; a world where Hong Kong housewives gamble away their marketing money on the HKSE;

a world where American TV-anchorwomen almost give birth during live transmission; a world where Malay soap operas are so *sloooow* you fall asleep before they start sobbing and saying "*Sayang jangan tinggalkan aku*"; a world where evil *towkays* entrap innocent karaoke singers from Jinjang in vice and prostitution;

a world where Tamil heroes brush their teeth instead of kissing their girlfriends; a world where the fat Kapoor brothers still get the leading roles; a world where Do Re Mi doesn't mean Julie Andrews, singing nuns and the hills are alive with the *Sound of Music*; a world where Anita Mui is still performing her last ultimate supreme final goodbye farewell show;

a world where dancers dance but never do high kicks and singers screech and sometimes hit the right notes; a world where every female presenter except Tunku Elida Bustaman wants to be Wan Zaleha (please come back, all is forgiven); a world where *Sejahtera Malaysia* leaves me (and you, go on, admit it) in patriotic tears if only because Elaine Kang's *cheongsam* looks as if it is a prototype for *Star Trek: The Next Generation*.

Celluloid reality seeps into your every crevice – your eyes, your ears, everywhere. Hell, you can shop by TV or call up that lovely Christine Ling on *Nona* and tell her exactly what you think about lime green pandan cakes. Of course, when you start thinking Jackie Eu should be nominated for the Oscars, you know you're a gonner – swamped and ready for Tanjong Rambutan. It's about this stage that you start dreaming of 'Movie Magic', '*Gaya Mutu Keunggulan*', amazing carpet cleaners for only RM5.99 and 'Films of exceptional quality' (who are they kidding?).

So what's so special about my celluloid reality? Special? It's all so marvellously special: that's what's special and I'm not kidding because I love it. What other reality is so diverse, so crazy, so funny, so bad (watch a *Cerekarama* if you don't believe me) and ultimately so Malaysian. Our TV, more than anything else in this crazy country, truly reflects what a quixotic and bizarre place we really live in. Where else in the world do you get television news in four languages as well as the weather in Mecca, Kota Bharu, Johannesburg, Paris and Sandakan?

I used to think of Malaysian TV as being hopelessly parochial and second rate. I was right about one thing: most of the time, it is second rate, at least in terms of production values, writing and acting. Some might say that that doesn't leave much, but despite all its failings, it's still effortlessly Malaysian: *rojak*, multiracial and cheery, so cheery that in *Pi Mai Pi Mai Tang Tu* you have turn down the volume or your eardrums will be damaged. Then there are moments of inspired TV, moments that make you proud and pleased to be a Malaysian, such as when Suhaimi Sulaiman asked the IGP's nine-year-old daughter what her father was really like. I remember thinking at the time that Malaysia can't be too bad if we allow our TV cameras right into the IGP's house and then quiz his daughter on his behaviour. Talk about aggressive interviewing. That, and *Melodi's* interviews with prominent hypocrites, all goes to make great viewing.

Malaysian TV may still have a long, long way to go – a little editorial independence wouldn't be a bad idea – but nonetheless, it's heading in the right direction. It is, at times, fast, funny and very Malaysian. Now, if only I could figure out how to switch the wretched TV off. If you don't believe me, you should watch Ogy Ahmad Daud's *Melodi* on a Sunday morning.

Ruling With Aplomb

The Sun: Ceritalah
25 February 1995

Philosophers, princes and prophets have always been concerned with the way man has tried to govern himself. Each in turn has suggested ways and means of ordering society. In the past, we in Asia would have looked to Plato, de Tocqueville, Marx and Milton Friedman for guidance in the belief that everything that came out of the citadels of Europe and America had to be right because they – the *Mat Sallehs* – were taller, whiter and had bigger noses. Nowadays, it's become just as fashionable to decry the West and disparage the writings we once adulated because the same people are suddenly lazier, stupider (because they've got big noses) and more barbaric than we at first realised.

Anyhow, with an election bearing down on us, I felt it was time to start looking over the great Asian canon of philosophy and, of course, the *Koran*. Why? Well, perhaps because it would suggest a way to exercise my constitutional right to vote.

Unfortunately, the institution of democracy and popular elections were not present either in 7th-century Arabia or the China of Confucius and Mencius. Because of this, I was forced to draw analogies. What do I mean? Well, I mean I was forced to read with half a mind on the underlying principles and meaning as well as their applicability to modern-day society – in a sense, a kind of *ijtihad*, a kind of reinterpreting that was both dynamic and ambitious without losing sight of the original.

So, what in particular drew my attention? Quite simply, the definitions. Definitions? Am I being pedantic? Well, in true *ceritalah* style: yes and no. For example, in Confucius' *Analects*, I was drawn to the philosopher's principle of the rectification of names, which was all about the definitions we attach to things. According to Confucius, if I'm not mistaken, the argument runs as follows: every thing or object possesses a particular characteristic that is the essence of that thing. Sorry about the doublespeak but let me explain further. Basically, a ruler or king has a certain characteristic or essence; in Confucius' scheme of things, a 'way' which is both righteous (*yi*) and human-hearted (*jen*) as well as imbued with certain responsibilities and duties. For example, Confucius says quite simply: "Let the ruler be ruler, the minister minister, the father father and the son son."

Enigmatic? Yes and no – because it does suggest a way of looking at the world, our institutions of state and our ministers that is disarmingly straightforward. Observe them, he seems to be saying, and see how well they match up to what they are supposed to be. We should be asking, how righteous or human-hearted have our leaders been in the execution of their duties? Have they sought private profit – contemptible, at least in Confucious' eyes?

The *Koran* and the *Hadiths* are very similar. The emphasis once again is on the definition of what constitutes a good ruler and how the 'actual' ruler measures up to the ideal. Obedience, the *Koran* cautions, is only due to those who are truly good: a salutary thought for some politicians. Thus whilst someone may be the ruler, his or her failure to rule well renders him or her, no longer worthy of that position. As with Confucius, there is argument that there is such a thing as an 'ideal' ruler and that the 'actual' ruler had better watch out because his performance is being judged.

There is also a call for men of authority to exercise that authority sparingly and wisely for the good of the community as a whole rather than in their own interests. One *hadith*, in particular, captured the breadth of the responsibility a ruler bore and its similarity to that of a father. So neat and engaging was its argument that I've chosen to quote it, in its entirety:

"Everyone of you is a ruler and every one of you shall be questioned about those under his rule; the king is a ruler and he shall be

questioned about his subjects; and the man is a ruler in his family and he shall be questioned about those under his care; and the woman is a ruler in the house of her husband, and she shall be questioned about those under her care; and the servant is a ruler in so far as the property of his master is concerned, and he shall be questioned about that which is entrusted to him."

So what did my reading teach me? Well, it taught me that whilst we may be in the process of dispensing with the works of the West, those of the East are just as trenchant in their criticisms of corruption, autocracy and misgovernment. In fact I felt that the measure by which we should judge our political 'masters' had become more stringent than anything that existed hitherto. I now wonder whether our political 'masters' realise what they've let themselves in for?

Political Life

Framing The Body Politic

The Sun: Ceritalah
1 April 1995

The row over Flor Contemplacion reminds me of a *jerawat* I once had on the end of my nose – it was so large and full of pus I couldn't face going out. And because I was so self-conscious about it (it was very large), I was extremely defensive when in company, blaming everybody else for my acne. Of course, that's not to say I didn't stop eating *goreng pisang*, chocolate and other greasy, fatty foods.

What connection does the spot on my nose have with the unfortunate Flor? First of all, the spot started out as nothing more than a simple blackhead. Unfortunately, it was teased and pressed almost absent-mindedly into a monster of a *jerawat*. It grew so large that it became an embarrassment. Sounds crude, doesn't it? Even a bit distasteful, huh? Well, that's intentional, because the Flor Contemplacion incident is as unsightly as fully-blown acne on the end of your nose and just about as important. Because, as we all know, acne doesn't necessarily leave any physical scars – something the Filipinos, in their haste and unnecessary emotionalism, have overlooked.

If the Flor Contemplacion incident was the *jerawat* on the Filipino body politic, then I'd be forced to say that the body politic – the nation itself – was not in very good health. Why? The list of contributing factors is endless. Any half-competent dermatologist would be able to see that. For a start, there are the dirty hands of politicians (still grubby from counting the US dollars they've deposited in Hong Kong and LA), the insubstantial diet, the squalor and filth of the housing, not to mention the hopelessness of living in a country where hard work, thrift and education may never lift you out of poverty.

By way of comparison, the Singaporean body politic is lean, muscular, tanned and healthy. Because of his sheer vitality (he undergoes regular training and work-outs because of his national service training), he's a little arrogant: arrogant in the way that good-looking rich people generally are. He's so healthy and categorical in his ways that others find him brash and insensitive. Some might even say he's got no personality but I'd say that that's going too far – I am sure he loves his mother.

He likes to do things by the book, forgetting that the point of the 'book' (it can also be called the rule of law) is that it should be adaptable to circumstance and human nature. His gestures are ham-fisted because he doesn't understand the importance of humility. This is a shame because the very rich should never forget that they share the world with those less fortunate than themselves. Consequently, it's beholden on the rich and the strong to be a little indulgent and accommodating with their weaker, troubled neighbours.

Now, everyone knows that psychological problems can make acne worse and I'm afraid the Singaporean disregard for the Filipino body politic has done just that: make the problem worse. By ignoring public opinion, the Singaporean inadvertently spurred the Filipino on to meddle with his irritating spot. And, of course, its location at the end of the nose means that the Filipino can't look anywhere without seeing the wretched *jerawat*.

The Filipino body politic is a sorry sight. Whole chunks of the body are missing. It's almost as if he's contracted leprosy. This is a damning indictment of his country because leprosy is a disease that modern medicine can cure. Nonetheless, his features and his limbs bear all the hallmarks of leprosy's ravages. The leprosy is a reflection of the fact that hundreds of thousands of his most productive cells (his impoverished people) are living outside his body whilst a few very greedy parts of his body – the stomach and the brain – live very well as politicians, landowners and industrialists enjoy themselves, gorging themselves without a thought for the poor and downtrodden.

The absence of all these productive cells and the imbalance between the different parts makes the Filipino irrational and emotional: the opposite of his Singaporean counterpart who is a monster of 'reason'. His pride is more easily dented because he knows he's in such a desperate situation. And yet, almost pathetically, he possesses glorious memories – the '50s when he was the lean, athletic young man on the block and the triumphs of '86 and Peoples' Power when, even though he was frail, his spirit was intact, proud and confident.

Long after Flor Contemplacion has been forgotten, we in ASEAN will be left sharing the 'block' with an emaciated and befuddled Filipino – someone who reminds us of the mad man sitting on the rubbish at the Chow Kit market. Treating him with disdain is no solution. He doesn't need help, he needs friendship – something that will make him want to join the community of nations. However, he'll never recover his health until he, himself, acts. He must seize hold of himself, re-gather his lost cells and learn to live for the good of every Filipino and not just the scabrous, self-important filth that call themselves the Filipino political and business elite – men and women who have, through their corruption and evil (because bad government is evil), reduced the Philippine nation single-handedly to a half-living cadaver scouring the dung-heaps of Asia.

The Lust Of Betrayal

The Sun: Ceritalah
24 September 1995

While the Tan Sri Rahim Thamby Chik case has left an unpleasant taste in the mouth, it would be wrong not to draw some conclusions from the experience as a whole. There are two points that have sprung to mind in the past few weeks, amidst the recriminations and the sleaze. The first is that politicians have to learn to live their lives 'better' then the rest of the population at large. The second is that no one is above the law.

This may seem obvious. Unfortunately, it is not and there's no harm repeating it: no one is above the law. Politicians have to bear in mind that they are not just private citizens. They are public property. Having elected a man or woman into office, we always have the right to expect more of them than we do of ourselves. If you want people to vote for you, you must be sure that you are special – and you then have to be able to live according to that 'special' yardstick.

Let me explain further. When I entrust someone with a duty – whatever that duty may be – they have to fulfil it. If they fail, they have betrayed my trust and the failure is all the worse for that. Think of an election as a process whereby a few thousand people entrust, say Rahim, with a duty – a duty to govern the state of Malacca. Alright, that's quite simple. But tens of thousands of people's trust has now been broken. I should add that Rahim has not been charged or tried as yet and therefore he's still innocent until proven guilty of an offence.

Nonetheless, as a politician who has been elected by thousands, he's entrusted with a duty not to allow his life or his name to be tainted by sleaze. When you also consider that thousands of Umno Youth supporters also supported him, the scale of the betrayal looms even larger.

You could argue that Rahim was not entrusted with a duty not to have a relationship with a 15-year-old girl. That's a fair point. If you look on the ballot papers, it says nothing about your views on the candidate's sexual proclivities. But if he's proven to have had the relationship with the girl (an important proviso), he has still broken the bond that exists between the electorate and the elected.

He was elected into office on the unwritten understanding that he would uphold and enforce the laws, customs and *adat* of the country. Entrusted with their enforcement, he's expected to be the most rigorous in adhering to them in the first place. He, the elected person, must lead by example. But more importantly, a leader is expected to live a life somewhat separate and better that those he governs. He or she should encapsulate our hopes. A leader must be a better man or woman in some vital respect. Despite all these qualities, they must also come to governance with clean hands. That is an imperative.

Human frailties are all very well … occasionally. But the dereliction of duty that Rahim is alleged to have shown is out of the question. Political figures are a kind of projection of ourselves. We vote for them because they are what we want to see the country becoming: they are our future. When they betray that trust and abuse it, they are abusing our notion of who we are as Malaysians. We don't want to be ruled by crooks, pimps and thieves; as such, we endeavour not to vote them into power (though it has been known to happen). When a man turns into a crook on being elected, the betrayal is terrible and his just desserts are ignominy and condemnation.

A man who is a leader has to be able to command the genuine admiration of the people. Can Rahim Thamby Chik really have been aware of all those people who voted for him in Masjid Tanah, his constituency? Can he have been aware of the trust that he has abused? Wasn't he concerned with how people would judge him?

Did he care?

The most important lesson is that no one, however powerful or wealthy, is above the law. The nation is built on a social contract: I, a citizen, contract to obey all the laws duly passed by the country's elected legislators. They, in turn, must administer those laws fairly in return. In short, no funny business.

If they fail to administer the laws or are partial to one of their number, the whole edifice runs the risk of being corrupted. In time, constant infractions may mean that the edifice will collapse. All of us must stand up against such an eventuality. If we don't, there will be no justice – only thuggery.

I paint a harsh picture because the rule of law is central to our lives. If people know they can break the laws of the land – then escape punishment – we will end up with a position much like present-day Philippines where the man with the gun is king. As such, it's imperative that Rahim's case is subjected to the most scrupulous research. No stone must go unturned. Having risen so high in the political spectrum, his fall will be painful. I'm sorry for that and for his family. However, that doesn't obscure the fact that justice must be done and must be seen to be done.

Rahim was wrong when he said to the press that his fate rested on the word of one man – implying that the PM could choose to do whatever he wanted with him. That was wrong. Only the law can decide Rahim's fate. As a journalist, I can speculate but I cannot judge. The judges must judge, and in their judging, they, too, must be fair and equal.

The Remains Of The Day

The Sun: Ceritalah
20 May 1995

Over the past few months, I have discovered just how conservative my views on life, political or otherwise, truly are. For a start, the ten days I spent covering the election soon doused the liberal flames raging in my heart. As one journalist said to me of my election coverage: "Karim, you scuttled out of your privileged rabbit-hole, shat and dashed back in again."

All this has to do with the debt I – a wealthy, educated Malay – owe my nation. I cannot deny the fact of this debt – and any Malay who says otherwise is lying. The assistance (moral, political and financial) that I have received over the years makes me both indebted and perhaps more importantly, somehow responsible.

However, as a writer, I'm forced to tussle both with this responsibility and a changing world, a world where the verities I grew up with – those democratic, liberal ones – are no longer valid. Quite frankly, all this worries me because I like certainty. I know that I should be trying to formulate or categorise the new Asian paradigm and I will try.

But for now, at least, I'll be doing most of the 'thinking' in the privacy of my own mind. I think it's only fair if I give you, the reader, a sense of the responsibility I feel I bear. Perhaps you'll understand? Or maybe you'll think I'm self-deluded? Whatever it is, I'll leave it to you to decide.

A few weeks ago, I held a cocktail party to celebrate the launch of a business I'd started with a partner who bore the striking, if unusual, name of Caesar. The reception was your standard KL yuppie 'bash': the beer flowed, the staff laughed, the unmarried guests chatted up one another whilst pretending to do business and I lost count of how many people I shook hands with. Two days later, I was still plucking namecards out of my trouser turn-ups – but that's another story and I won't go into it now.

Amidst all the noise and shrieks of old friends who hadn't seen each other for years – *'Lamaaaa tak jumpaaa'* – a small, sprightly older man arrived at the office. As he stood in the reception area patiently, I wondered what must have been going through his mind. His name was Hanafiah Hussain – Dato' Hanafiah. Whilst it might not mean much to anyone else, he had once been my father's partner in a business venture – an accountancy practice – that the two men had launched well over 30 years before. Dato' Hanafiah, amongst many other things, had been an accountant, a banker, a publisher and a politician.

In those days, he had been a man on the rise – a man to look out for (promise that was borne out by his long and illustrious career). He had been the MP for Jerai, in a Dewan Rakyat so packed with personality and potential that every Dewan Rakyat since seems a mere shadow. Just to list the names – some resonant with history – seems unbelievable enough: Lee Kuan Yew, Nik Kamil, the Seenivasagam brothers, Joe Manjaji, Temenggong Jugah, Tunku Abdullah.

I strode up to greet him and was struck almost immediately by the look of quiet, unspoken pride on his face.

"To think," he said to me at once, his eyes moist with emotion, "that you were so small when your father and I set up HRM. And now here I am at your launch party. How time passes! It's your time now, you know, you young people. It's your time now."

Dato' Hanafiah left soon after. I don't think I'll forget Dato' Hanafiah's warmth that day. In this day and age when we Malays are supposed to be so calculating and mercenary, I must confess it was the older man's presence at the reception that gave me more satisfaction than any number of wealthy bankers.

I am writing these things now because I want to explain how important the past or at least a sense of one's own personal history is to the present. The older man signified a link with the past – a link with the world I come from and the world to which I owe my dues. Hanafiah Raslan Mohamad – their firm – was a product of the Malay push into the business world. And whilst business conditions have changed substantially over the decades, I am still, to all intents and purposes, a product of the same push. I can never deny this truth – nor would I ever want to.

Having said all this, having admitted my debt to the political world that nurtured and created my class, I have to admit that I – like many others of my generation – feel that there are different challenges ahead of us. And it is about tackling these challenges and the changes that my class must endure, that my silent thoughts must turn.

A Corruption Of Ideals

The Sun: Ceritalah
24 December 1995

I've been very disappointed by the recent disclosures about the way Bumiputra share allocations (for KLSE-listed companies) are made and to whom. I should add that I say 'disappointed' and not shocked because the ins-and-outs of the allocations have long been a subject of keen interest in KL's corporate circles. Everyone seems to know – or rather they profess to know – who got the Bumiputra allocations for a whole slew of KLSE-listed companies and, more importantly, why they got the allocations. I'll leave you to figure out what the various beneficiaries may or may not have done to deserve the allocations. Business gossip aside, the episode has revealed some curious aspects about Malaysian society, public morality and our leaders.

First of all, I should stress that the Bumiputra allocations that have recently come under public scrutiny are not, strictly speaking, incidents of corruption. Nothing about them is illegal – at least as far as I know. Which begs the question – why has the episode left me with an unpleasant taste in the mouth? It's not illegal. Well, I think it's because it reveals one of those worrying areas of public life where morality and the law are not in 'sync', an area where the laws are behind public morality.

Public morality would prefer it if the families of prominent politicians did not receive Bumiputra share allocations. I've heard many reasons why the family members were included but I'm sorry to say that none of them satisfy me. To my mind, the business of government must at all costs be seen to be fair and above board. These kinds of shenanigans are just not right – *tidak manis*, *tidak ngam*.

However, I may be alone in thinking this because I've found that very few people seem to give a damn. It's as if the public at large has such a low opinion of Malaysian politicians that the disclosures are irrelevant. One broker told me, "Who gives a °°°° about a few million ringgit? Anyhow, if I could, I would give all the shares to my family." Strangely, the allocations, their size and their beneficiaries seem to be a relative non-event in newspaper terms. Public outcry, maybe? Well, no – forget it, not even a blip.

The absence of interest puzzles me. I think Malaysians should be more concerned. As Malaysia becomes more and more middle class, such distasteful antics should also become intolerable. Why? Well, a prosperous and contented middle class requires a Government that is clean, straight-dealing, accountable and transparent. Remember *'bersih, cekap dan amanah'*?

The middle class needs to know that their thrift, their salaried jobs and their hard work will not be overwhelmed by corruption, cronyism and sleaze. Most members of the middle class do not have access to politicians: they have to trust in their elected representatives, depending on their fairness and honesty. If, as in black Africa and the Philippines, they lose confidence in the Government, the society as a whole loses a vital prop to stability and prosperity – people grow wary of saving, fearful of the future, distrustful of Government and corruption shoots up even more.

I feel that in Malaysia our citizenry may be in danger of taking its lead from the leadership, a leadership that seems to be growing more amoral and uninterested in public opinion as the years progress. Is this leadership by example? Our middle class is becoming so habituated to shady antics that it can't be bothered to protest. As a result, our citizenry is both supine and amoral. Could it be that an absence of public morality is one of these much vaunted Asian values? I sure as well hope not!

The more I thought about these allocations, the more I wondered how we could avoid such incidents in the future. Perhaps our politicians aren't being rewarded well enough? No, don't laugh, I'm being serious. In Singapore, for example, Cabinet Ministers earn salaries on par with the private sector. Should Malaysia follow suit?

Ministers are expected to manage vast sums of money for a pittance. Such responsibility requires men and women of high calibre: pay peanuts and you get monkeys. Would higher pay make a difference? Would that also have prevented the incidents that Rahim, for example, now stands accused of?

As I tried to figure out what I really thought about the allocations, I knew I had to concede one point – their original purpose and intention was vital. The allocations were intended to help Malays accumulate capital, pulling them out of the kampungs and into the cities and boardrooms. It was the central feature of the country's political and economic stability.

Having faced up to the historical realities, I started wondering about whether or not these realities had remained the same. For a start, I would hesitate to describe the beneficiaries of the Bumiputra allocations as the most needy section of the Malay community. But most importantly, I have to confess that the political and economic realities have changed: the Malaysia of 1994 is very different from the Malaysia of 1971. Could it be that the necessities of 1971 are no longer necessities today?

The Landed Gentry

The Sun: Ceritalah
11 March 1995

Earlier this year, a Kadazan friend of mine living in KL approached a property company and asked them whether or not they had any properties for sale in a particular development that had caught her eye. When the reply was in the affirmative, she asked if there were any Bumiputra lots still available. She was told that yes, there were but that no, they weren't available for her. She, quite rightly, asked them why not. They replied that the Bumiputra lots were only to be sold to Muslim Malay Bumiputras.

This story rather surprised me because as far as I knew, there was only one kind of Bumiputra and he or she was defined clearly according to the Federal Constitution. However, in my naivete, I had failed to factor in the very real prejudices still at work in Malaysia. As a result, I decided to find out a little more. First of all, I referred to that barometer of the social and economic mix, the KLSE Handbook, searching for any prominent non-Muslim Bumiputra Sabahan or even Sarawakian directors. To my dismay, I couldn't seem to find any. However, I may have overlooked some names because in Sabah, for example, many people with Chinese-sounding names are, in fact, Bumiputras by dint of possessing at least one Kadazan or other native grandparent.

Since I have quite a few Sabahan and Sarawakian friends, I asked them whether or not they'd experienced similar examples of prejudice and to my surprise and shame – because I am a Muslim Malay Bumiputra – they had. And I use the word 'shame' advisedly because I felt – just as every other Muslim Malay Bumiputra should feel – personally tainted and partly responsible for the shoddy treatment they received. I realised that what my friend had endured at the hands of a surly property salesperson was not a coincidence.

This was all the more disturbing when one considers the high hopes with which UMNO first ventured into Sabah and the subsequent electoral victory (albeit marred by accusations of bribery and corruption). The fact remains that most Sabahans, whether Muslim or non-Muslim Bumiputra, still feel that they are at the mercy of powerful peninsular Malaysia prejudices. It strikes me as worrying that we should be unable to stamp out such prejudice, if only because it lies at the root of PBS's support. If UMNO is serious about its long-term future in Sabah, this kind of prejudice, quite frankly, has to go.

We have to learn to treat the Sabahans, of all religions, as equals. If we don't, we will fail to gain their support and confidence, pushing them back into PBS's embrace. Moreover, the Malay Bumiputras, of which I am one (and a very privileged one), should, by now, be in the position to act with a degree of magnanimity. We Malays control the levers of business and government: to deny that is to deny the truth. Given this, a wise leader will surely see that he needs to relinquish some of that power and authority, empowering and benefiting others in turn.

Furthermore, the underlying purpose of the NEP, as I see it, is the redressing of age-old economic and social ills. As such, it is intended to benefit all Bumiputras, who in the main, suffered equally badly under the benign neglect of the British, whether in the Raja Brooke's Sarawak, the North Borneo Company or the peninsula. As a son of a prime architect of the NEP, I have long had my personal qualms about it – qualms about its implementation and direction which I have voiced time and again.

However, in the case of the Bumiputras in Sabah and Sarawak, the continued implementation of the NEP is crucial. They remain an overlooked section of modern Malaysia. During my years travelling as a freelance journalist in East Malaysia, I have witnessed economic and social conditions that are as bad, if not worse, than the very worst the peninsula has to offer.

I can still recall the acrid squalor of the squatter settlement at Pujut Lima in Miri, a shanty town (inhabited by Kayan, Kenyah and Iban in the main) balanced precariously on human excrement, plastic bags and sawmill off-cuts where cheap, foul-smelling rice wine dispensed from makeshift huts provided just about the only solace. Rural poverty according to these slum-dwellers was even worse. At least in the towns, their children had access to schools and clinics. Driving across Sabah from Kota Kinabalu to Tawau, I was later to see that rural Sabah is, indeed, in an appalling condition – a condition that requires more assistance rather than less. The Bumiputras, both Muslim and non-Muslim, in Sabah and Sarawak are the black spot of the NEP and should remain on all our consciences until something more positive is done.

Anwar Ibrahim

Men's Review
November 1993

Dato' Seri Anwar has been a very busy man. In the past weeks, he has crossed the globe to attend the World Bank/IMF Conference in Washington, as well as touring the various UMNO Divisions through-out the country, meeting with key decision-makers in each of the states. Constant movement and activity have long been an integral part of Anwar's way of life. Even in the late '70s when V. S. Naipaul was conducting research for his book *Among the Believers*, he commented on Anwar's peripatetic existence and the various demands on his time.

"I would have liked to talk more with Anwar. It occurred to me, after our first meeting in the ABIM office, that I should travel about Malaysia with him, and see the country through his eyes. He was willing; but it didn't work out. He was busy, at the centre of all the ABIM activity; he was constantly on the move, by car and plane: he was in demand as an orator," said Naipaul.

With his emotion-charged candidacy announced at a packed press conference on August 25 this year, Anwar has had to maintain political momentum right up to November's vital party polls. This, in turn, has made the travelling all the more important.

Whilst the struggle for Deputy President with Ghafar Baba may not be over, there was a growing feeling (even in early October) that Anwar's candidacy would triumph. As one Division Youth Head said, "It's settled, as far as I'm concerned: Anwar's the successor. We'd better get used to it." Such views have been an anathema to Ghafar's camp where the contest has been taken very seriously, notwithstand-ing all the setbacks.

As more and more people have been talking about the 'inevita-bility' of an Anwar victory, as opposed to the 'possibility', attention has shifted to the man himself. It is trite to say that Anwar is an enigma: everyone says that, as if being an enigma is an answer in itself – some kind of solution to the complexity of his personality. Such arguments are usually followed by a recitation of his entry into politics in 1982, his 'outsider' status followed by his supercharged career to date (Minister of Culture, Youth and Sports, Minister of Education and now the Finance Ministry). Rehman Rashid, the noted writer, sees Anwar differently.

"The signal difference between Dr Mahathir and Anwar is that Anwar is more a representation of his generation, a hologram, if you like, of his generation and all their aspirations. He is defined by his generation and, like them, he is still in the process of growing and developing."

Nonetheless, the uncertainty still persists. As one businessman said, "I don't know what he stands for. I don't know if he still espouses his views from the '70s. At the end of the day, he's different from so many of the other UMNO politicians because of his depth of character and the breadth of his experience and reading. How many members of the Government have been detained for their views? It's just that I don't know what he really thinks."

Anwar is, and continues to be, well-read (he has been known to quote Umberto Eco and Durkheim in political speeches), a fact that one does not normally associate with the UMNO elite, many of whom have eschewed the intellectual arena. Despite his heavy workload, Anwar still finds time to read and one cosmopolitan Tan Sri was recently surprised to find that Anwar had read the Nigerian-born Booker Prize-winning novelist Ben Okri's work.

Meeting the man in person, I was struck, like V. S. Naipaul before me, by his personal charm and attractiveness. It is the charm of a reflective, man, thoughtful and reticent but winning nonetheless. As one foreign journalist says, "to be honest, he has us eating out of his hands." However, the problem with charm and those who possess it in abundance (and Anwar most definitely does: he makes one feel at ease almost immediately) is that it glosses over the intricacies of a man's character. Part of his charm lies in the way it suggests that he is still learning, still feeling his way through the complex problems of Governance, Islam and Development – in short, the big questions facing any Malaysian leader.

But his charm has been a double-edged sword. He is surprisingly affable and wide-ranging (horse-riding to scuba-diving) in his interests, and because of this, it has been difficult for people to pigeonhole him. As he says himself, "I have been accused of being too close to the Chinese *towkays* and too liberal on the one hand, and a Muslim extremist on the other. Often, when people meet me, they are surprised that I laugh, but I do. I think they think I'm some extraterrestrial. For example, when I scuba dive, people expect me to dive down to 200 feet because of who I am."

I may appear to have overemphasised the issue of character and personality, but judging by anecdotal evidence, the majority of Malaysians are just as keen to 'figure out' the man behind the Minister. In short, our leaders set the tone of government. Their concerns, whilst reflecting the nation at large, are determined by personal factors largely beyond our knowledge. For example, it seems unlikely that the country would have launched into a policy of rapid industrialisation had it not been for Dr Mahathir's drive.

As one middle-class Malay says, "Anwar is like Dr Mahathir in that he is a man with ideas. He has, I think, an agenda, though I'm not too sure what it is."

Part of the uncertainty lies in Anwar's pre-1982 political career. In the 1970s when he was a student at University of Malaya, he was an outspoken and charismatic political activist. Hard-hitting in his criticism of Government, of corruption, hypocrisy and poverty, he tapped a rich seam of social and political discontent that appeared to have parallels with Iran and the Middle East – a seam that Naipaul mined in his highly-praised book. During his years with ABIM, the Malaysian Muslim Youth Movement, he attracted a loyal band of supporters, many of whom have followed him into the UMNO fold. When asked about his days in ABIM, he stresses the generational aspect of his concerns, answering, "You must remember that in the '70s, every young Malay man was an activist. The '80s and '90s have been very different."

Nonetheless, the legacy of those years remains at the back of many people's minds. It has been a kind of 'bogey' that has confused people's perception of Anwar, introducing questions such as "Does he want to Islamicize the economic system? And if so, how does he intend to do it?" into any discussion of Anwar.

There has been a tendency to overplay his 'outsider' status by his detractors, without giving due regard to Anwar's equally strong 'establishment' ties. His father was a two-term National Front MP from Penang – hardly an indication of poverty or social alienation. Besides that, Anwar is also a product of the Malay College Kuala Kangsar, a connection that many younger businessmen are keen to foster. The MCKK connection could perhaps be seen as a bulwark to his subsequent ABIM years.

I must confess that a 40-minute interview is hardly very much to go on. And secondly, that journalists, especially those such as myself who like to consider ourselves as 'thinkers' as well, leap at the opportunity of interviewing Anwar. We are human too and we're also dazzled and refreshed by the erudition, the charm and the good looks.

Despite his persuasiveness in person, Anwar was at pains to stress that his actions should speak for themselves: "I think people should look more closely at my policies and what I have implemented rather than get swept up into loose speculation. For example, during my tenure in the Education Ministry, I initiated and pushed for the return of English Literature teaching – not something that people would commonly associate with me." In the same way, he adds, "I should be judged on the basis of my stewardship of the economy."

Whilst there are many who would say, as one Chief Executive did to me, "Anwar inherited the present economic boom from his predecessor Tun Daim," others have argued that the art of non-intervention in the economy is just as important as the art of intervention. One security analyst went so far as to say, "Anwar should be commended for the way he has maintained current government policies without trying to revamp and change everything."

And the figures have vindicated him – Anwar's prudent steering of the economy has paid dividends. Second Quarter GDP results featured 10.4% growth and only 3.5% inflation, figures that were favourably received by the financial community. On the back of such figures and strong American institutional interest, the KLSE has also been notching up record gains.

And he stressed at the interview, "Growth is my biggest concern. Only through growth can we have equity and a better standard of living for everybody."

Poverty and its eradication, through education and economic growth, are very much the central planks of Dr Mahathir's policies and Anwar seeks to show his congruence with the Prime Minister's thinking. As another prominent Malaysian politician says of Anwar, "The (economic) policies are already in place. The personalities may change as politicians come and go but the Government will not waver in its direction. Anwar is part of the continuity and stability in Malaysian Government – he is not a break."

To my mind, one of the strongest strands in Anwar's political career has been his commitment to eradicating poverty and improving education. As he says of Malaysia, "The uniqueness of the Malaysian experience has been that growth has always been bound up with a very caring society. Progress is quite even, though there are noteworthy exceptions in Sabah, Sarawak and the east coast of the Peninsula. But the improvements in services can only be achieved in tandem with economic growth." Anwar's commitment to economic growth is wholehearted. And I would suggest that it is this commitment that will militate against the introduction of any policies that threaten our hard-earned prosperity.

But as Malaysia has grown more prosperous, there has been a growing need to consider the less well-favoured members of our society.

"The country," he says, "must have some form of social agenda. We don't have the resources to solve the problems of the Indian estate labourers or the urban poor at the moment. There's nothing socialistic or radical in trying to alleviate these problems. But the Government has some basic principles, and I think a laissez-faire economy with minimum regulation can be encouraged to tackle these issues. A failure to do so would result in a social riot."

It is possible that Anwar, now 47, is an example of youthful idealism tempered by experience. In the past, he might have been more radical and outspoken, but now, fully apprised of the complexity of governance, he has seen the need for consensus and compromise. As another political observer says, "Dr Mahathir was also thought of as an extremist, even a racist, in his earlier days. But look at his performance to date – the critics have been proved entirely wrong. The Malaysian system ensures that the leaders 'grow' into their jobs: there's no John Major-like leap from the unknown. The Malaysian system irons out the glitches."

Nonetheless, concerns about his intentions still persist and political commentators have pointed to the ease with which he has appeared to have sidelined Ghafar Baba in the contest for UMNO Deputy President. Despite the fact that he is the challenger, the perception, at least among many of the UMNO faithful, is the reverse. He has turned the tables on the incumbent and then dictated the terms of the political debate.

Under the newly-revised UMNO Constitution, the selection of UMNO President and Deputy President are no longer straightforward electoral contests. Each Division is empowered to nominate one person for either post and, having done so, the recipient is entitled to an extra 10 electoral votes per nomination received. In short, what this means is that the contests for the top two posts in the party can be resolved by the simple expedient of one candidate collecting a clear majority on the back of the divisional nominations.

In practice, this has meant that the incumbent is normally in the stronger position vis-à-vis any challenger. Or at least this is what it once meant because Anwar Ibrahim's candidacy has overturned all previous assumptions.

The Finance Minister's well-run campaign has benefited from his greater understanding of the aspirations of many of the younger party members – Rehman's 'hologram' metaphor. Whilst he has managed to capture the minds of the Malay community, he has also emphasised the need for pluralism and a willingness to live with people of other cultures and religions. And these are not merely empty words because Malaysia is just such a success – a polity fuelled by economic growth where genuine multiculturalism has taken root.

Hisham Hussein Onn: The Son Also Rises

Men's Review
August 1994

On November 3, 1993, in a packed auditorium of the Putra World Trade Centre, during last year's UMNO General Assembly, a new, and yet familiar, face emerged onto the political arena, as the third generation of the Onn Jaafar family, Hishammuddin Hussein Onn, 32-year-old lawyer-businessman, son of the former Prime Minister and grandson of the founder of UMNO, was elected to the UMNO Youth Exco, one of the first steps up the UMNO hierarchy.

The 1993 Assembly saw the UMNO faithful moving yet further away from the *cikgu*, or schoolteacher, activist roots of its past towards the new paradigm – the world of the professionals and businessmen, the much-vaunted *orang korporat* – the Melayu Baru, or the New Malay. As the party reinvented itself, reflecting the changes in the nation as a whole, Hisham's (most people call him Hisham) election – he polled the highest number of votes of all those elected to the Youth Exco – revealed an interesting aspect of UMNO's political culture: a reprise from the past, albeit in a different form. As one onlooker said, "The 'Onns' are Malaysia's equivalent of the Roosevelts."

"I think it would be true to say," Hisham said to me in an interview a few months after his election, "that I do feel at ease with the older values. It may sound trite, but I've always wanted to serve the public and it didn't necessarily have to be in politics.

"My parents brought us up with certain values and I am where I am now because of the support given to me by my family as well as the support from the party because of who I am. Therefore, I am responsible to the party for that vote of confidence."

I should add that I have known Hisham for many years. We practised law together at Skrine & Co in the late '80s. In those days,

I used to join him and his late father for lunch at the family home in Kenny Hills. There is an image of those lunches that will always remain in my mind and it is of the younger man kissing his father's hand, both as he arrived and left the house.

Such refinement and breeding struck me, a young pushy lawyer in those days, as distinctly old-world, unnecessary even. Now, with society changing so fast (perhaps too fast?), I am not so sure. Maybe there is still a need for such things. Maybe their preservation is actually important. He entered active politics only four years ago, soon after his father's death. In that time, he has gone from being *anak Tun* or just 'the son of the late Tun' and an ordinary lawyer to a political and business 'player' in his own right – the kind of person that people want to get to know.

He has his own law firm, active business interests – a stake in the Second Board-listed construction firm Ekovest Bhd – as well an interest in Nanyang Bhd, the Chinese language newspaper group controlled by the Hong Leong Group. He is also reported to be a friend of the reclusive Hong Leong Group mastermind, Quek Leng Chan.

"With his father's death in 1989," said one ex-colleague, "the way seemed clear for him to enter the political fray. Hitherto, he had concentrated on his legal career." He chose to join an UMNO branch in Johor, rather than a KL branch, and with that he embarked on what was to be a regular weekly visit to the Ledang Division in northern Johor.

I followed Hisham down to Ledang one Friday and entered what was, for me at least, an entirely different world – albeit only minutes from the North-South highway. Having never grown up in a Malay kampung myself and only very irregularly visited one, the rush of faces, the hands ready to *salaam* and the general air of geniality was tiring, if not confusing.

We visited the house of the local State Assemblyman, YB Hashim Ismail, whose father had died the night before. Standing outside in the drizzling rain, I watched the candidate-to-be with his possible future constituents. To my surprise, I have to confess, he seemed to have an immediate rapport.

And, as everyone left, I watched almost in disbelief as he, cigarette in hand, hopped on the back on a motorbike and whizzed off into the distance. For all intents and purposes, the kampung folk treated him as one of their own and he, for his part, was entirely at ease. Considering that he had grown up in KL, in the midst of luxury and power, his ability to mix with all levels of society was eye-opening.

He lives in a three-storey terrace house in Ampang, is married to Tengku Marsilla, a Pahang princess, and has three young children. He and his young family were featured recently in the Malay woman's magazine *Nona*, a magazine whose distribution in the UMNO rural heartland is phenomenal. Though 32, his picture in the magazine makes him look much younger and with his attractive wife by his side, he must represent to many of *Nona's* readers, the Malay dream: wealth, position and class. Nonetheless, his concerns are, by way of contrast, down-to-earth.

"There's a lot that's very commendable about the kampung; the respect for the elders and the resilience of the family unit. Having said that, I can foresee problems in the future. As these communities grapple with the shift from rural to urban life, education, as always, is the key to the transition."

Many people I talked to who knew Hisham felt that, notwithstanding his name and lineage, he is an unlikely politician.

"He's too unassuming: politics in Malaysia is merciless," said one ex-colleague. And in truth, his character does seem at odds with the more aggressive, outspoken political culture of the present. Nonetheless, his rise has been stellar, so he must be doing something right.

"I have to admit there is an element of guilt in the way that I have risen so fast. I do feel it is kind of premature." Others have noted that his ingenuous public persona masks a steely political mind.

Whatever it is, he is the first to admit that he is not as widely read as he should be: "But I am an inquisitive person and I'll take every opportunity to dig for an answer: you can learn a lot by listening and observing people.

"Sincerity is the key to whatever you do: I have to evaluate people as I meet them, they have to evaluate me. People can tell pretty fast if you're not sincere."

He has projected the *berbudi bahasa* aspects of Malay culture and his family – the courtesy, the humility, the deference and the gentlemanliness – with such astuteness that he has ended up causing more waves than any number of hot-headed speakers.

"It's ironic," says another Johorean, "but Hisham's consensual approach and his very understatedness, all the things that the Melayu Baru rhetoric would have us disavow, may well be the key to his success. Maybe subliminally, the UMNO delegates were reaching out for the old ways." A Johorean politician ascribes his rise quite simply to his youth, saying, "He's so new to the game, he doesn't have any enemies, yet."

"His victory was based on sentiment alone," said one political analyst rather disdainfully. "The family name was what did it."

However, others have disagreed: "He wouldn't have risen so high if he was just riding his father's coat-tails (though it was an important motivator). He is more than just Tun Hussein's son. If he was campaigning purely on the basis of his name, he wouldn't have got anywhere."

There were still a number of unanswered questions in my mind about Hisham and I decided to attend a large, primarily Johorean function in KL recently, at which he spoke. It was an outdoor event and the crowd, as is often the case with such events, was more concerned with feeding themselves than listening to speeches. When Hisham stood up to speak, many people didn't really notice.

That's politics, I remember thinking to myself. I listened anyhow – it was my job to listen and since I was sitting next to the main audio-visual console, I ended up watching him speak on the TV screen, rather than in the flesh.

As I watched him on the TV screen, I realised that someone whom I had once thought of as an old friend had actually become someone quite different. TV refracts an individual, pushing into greater relief particular attributes and characteristics: he was a politician now and a cipher, a reflection of the society he represented, a focus for their hopes and aspirations.

What he represented – the marriage of old and new – was important. Whether he succeeded or not in the long run depended on the same forces within society – the old and the new, change and tradition – which had shaped him. To the onlooker, he seemed to have achieved a fine balance of the two at this very early stage of his career. The real test of his mettle would only come much later.

Troubled by these thoughts, I stopped a guy from the crowd and asked him about Hisham. "He is a qualified lawyer and a businessmen," the man answered. *Ada kelulusan*, or he has qualifications, was a phrase I kept on hearing. And then in a display of grassroots activism, he added firmly, "Anyhow, if a State Assemblyman or Member of Parliament doesn't deliver on his promises, we elect him out. It's not the old days anymore. All politicians have to listen to us, the people, now."

Politics is unforgiving and venturing into its murky waters is not easy for anyone. Birth may have given Hisham Hussein Onn a headstart. It is not an advantage that will last for very long. The promise will, no doubt, soon be put to the test and as Hisham said when we first talked, "At the end of the day, it's all up to the people. They will decide my future. I just have to be ready to serve."

People And Places

Taiping The Brave

The Sun: Ceritalah

11 February 1994

I've always thought of Taiping as a town so boring that the only source of excitement had to be either betting on the timing of the all-too-frequent rain showers or the various visitors to Kamunting: both short- and long-term. Coming from a family that liked to think of Kuala Kangsar down the road (or 'Kua-lleur' as we pronounced it) as their ancestral home, Taiping was always rather a joke – 'everlasting peace'? Forget it: more like everlasting tedium.

However, I should add that Taiping hasn't always been such a dead-end place. Reading Professor Khoo Kay Kim's delightful history of the town, I came across a whole host of strange stories and coincidences that seemed to pepper the town's genesis. For me, at least, they brought what I thought to be a rather dull place a little more to life.

First of all, there was the rise of the adventurer Long Ja'afar and his son Ngah Ibrahim. Such was their ambition and ability, they very nearly turned the area surrounding Taiping, called Larut, into their own personal kingdom. Then there were the incessant and bloody wars for the control of the area's great tin mining resources – full-scale wars between the rival Chinese gangs, the Teochew Ghi Hin and the Hokkien Hai San.

But best of all were the latter-day events – Pandit Nehru's visit in 1937 and his rapturous welcome by the town's Indian and Ceylonese communities. Then, in the dying days of the Second World War, the Indonesian leaders, Hatta and Soekarno, who stopped over at the town's airstrip briefly where they were greeted by the Malay nationalist leader Ibrahim Yaacob who unilaterally declared his allegiance to the concept of Indonesia Raya (thus swallowing what would have been Malaysia in one neat gulp).

Present-day Taiping seemed rather lifeless by comparison: a place to retire to and little else, as if the extraordinary Museum locked in its time-warp was the most telling metaphor for the town's present existence as a retirement home, a kind of Brighton-at-the-foot-of-the-Hill. Once again, however, I found myself proven wrong, learning something in the process about the quality of life outside of KL and the continuing, almost bizarre strangeness of this country when you least expect it.

It all started with a family wedding for which I made the mistake of arriving late, expecting there to be no traffic on streets of Taiping after 6 pm on a Saturday. Well, I was wrong, very wrong. Instead, I was enveloped by a cacophonous town whose streets were bustling and crowded with cars, motorbikes and shoppers on foot. Inching my way along the impressively named, but rather dismal, Jalan Kota, I scratched my head. Taiping? Traffic jams? What's going on?

Admittedly, it was a big wedding, at least in Taiping terms – the wedding of the eldest daughter of the local Orang Besar Jajahan, or Territorial Chief, the Tengku Mentri of Larut (the heirs to Ngah Ibrahim's patrimony), a title so redolent with history, verve and bravery that its continued existence in our more lacklustre age seemed curiously out-of-place.

Well, the wedding was just as I would have expected. I ended up sitting next to one busy-body *mak cik* who told me how many Tan Sris she was related to, the *real* sleeping partners of all of those just out of earshot, and the fact that her niece – a sweet bank manager – was still unmarried. Lucky me, heh? There was a table for the VIPS; the Sultan of Perak, the Raja Perempuan and the Raja Muda, all of whom watched the proceedings with a calm dispassionate air. Poor things, I remember thinking, they must sit through weddings like this night after night after night – a kind of living purgatory.

It was a noisy, colourful affair with singing – there was a tuneless *nasyid*, a lady's choir who gave a cheery but uninspiring version of *Joget Pahang* and a set of cultural dancers who smiled a lot and then darted from side to side with different fans and pieces of colourful nylon. And, as with all family weddings, there were uncles, aunts, great-aunts, great-great aunts, cousins, cousins and cousins – so many in fact, that you began to wonder who you weren't related to and how they managed to evade the clutches of your family.

After the wedding, we headed off for the newly opened Taiping Legend Inn. Now, I should add that the weekend of the wedding coincided with the presence of Joan Collins in KL at a similarly named hotel off Jalan Kuching, as opposed to this one, just off Jalan Kota, downtown Taiping.

Settling into the coffeeshop, I heard a young man at the reception asking for the august Alexis Carrington and shook my head – 'only in Taiping!'. By now, it was well past midnight and the hotel coffeeshop was beginning to take on the appearance of a Fellini stage set: you know, the kind of thing where anything can happen and anybody can just turn up as long as they're photographed for posterity by the silent cousin whose right hand is glued to an Olympus 'Mu' camera.

In retrospect, it must have seemed odd – there were all of us dressed up to the nines in our *baju melayu*, a prominent ABIM man whose name escaped me and his entourage, and many other wedding guests, Indian, Malay, Chinese and European as well as the bride and bridegroom who appeared from nowhere and then disappeared again. Suddenly, a set of double doors flew open and out thronged a host of MCA politicians led by Ling Liong Sik, all in white, hugging and back-slapping.

Hell, I thought, maybe the guy just now was right: maybe Joan Collins is staying here?

NEP Revisited

The Sun: Ceritalah
5 November 1994

I am a child of the NEP, a product of the social and economic policies first conceived and executed in the late sixties and seventies.
Without the existence of the NEP, it is highly unlikely that people
such as me – educated, middle-class Malays – would be around at
all. As a result, my debt to the NEP is total and I am forced to acknowledge it as such.

Nonetheless, this does not mean that I am without criticisms of
the policy. The NEP has cast such a long, and at times, not altogether happy shadow over Malaysian public life. For example, anything I achieve will always be clouded by the taint of tokenism and
favouritism. Unsurprisingly, it is not a subject that I enjoy discussing
at any great length with non-Malaysians because so few of them understand the constraints which led to the NEP's implementation.

This is why my recent visit to South Africa has come as such a
surprise. Here, in the southernmost tip of a troubled and bloody
continent, I came across countless very senior corporate executives
and consultants (mainly white, admittedly) who seemed to know a
great deal about the NEP, or the Bumiputra policy, as they preferred
to call it. Not only did they know about the NEP but they wanted to
know a whole lot more – bombarding me with questions about its
relative success, the equity requirements and educational achievements.

Why? Well, in retrospect, the parallels between the two countries are more numerous than they would seem at first instant. Most
importantly, both countries are multiracial. Secondly, the patterns
of development have long been skewered towards one particular
community at the expense of the majority. In the case of Malaysia,
most of the Malays were living in the rural areas, going to Malay

language schools – a world that was entirely apart and separate from the country's modern thriving economy. According to the 1947 census, only 38% of the population over 15 was literate.

Given the history of uneven development, the Malaysian government has achieved a near miracle. 1994 finds the literacy rate doubled to 78%. The Malay community has been empowered. Educated and hard-working, there are Malay doctors, lawyers, scientists and accountants, a vast middle class that has carpeted the Klang Valley with housing estates, golf courses and shopping centres. All this social engineering has been achieved without damaging the economy's essential ability to compete internationally.

So, is Malaysia is a blueprint for success? Well, for the South Africans, there aren't many other multiracial nations to look to. Yugoslavia? Rwanda? Nigeria? The other options are not very attractive. Malaysia, as one South African corporate man explained, is the only blueprint.

"I know that on paper, the Bumiputra policy sounds iniquitous and unfair but that's not the point. The point is, that it has succeeded. Theory and practice are often different. It's all very well to say something is fair and noble. However, such solutions often lead to chaos. And chaos serves no one's interests."

With a literacy rate of only 50%, a stalling economy and a black population segregated and sullen from decades of oppression, the South African elite, both political and business, have to act fast. The Reconstruction and Development Programme (RDP) put together by the ruling ANC is a noble and ambitious document. And, given South Africa's bloody recent history, the RDP is free of the animus that one might expect.

Unfortunately, the RDP is awash in 'rights' – the rights to water, land, women's rights, labour rights, etc. To be blunt, when you're planning to restructure a society, the centre needs power – naked power – and too much devolved power, especially to the unions, can wreak havoc. The unions are not concerned about South Africa's

40% unemployment. Unions only want to preserve the jobs of their members and South Africa happens to have wage rates (a US$250 minimum wage) far in excess of Malaysia without any commensurate increase in productivity. No multinational would invest in South Africa if this isn't resolved.

Another point is that the RDP promises too much too soon. A large black middle class – the one thing that will bring real peace and stability to South Africa – will take far longer to emerge than the five years of ANC's term of government. Education is the key. Unfortunately, the ANC is now suffering from its school boycott policies of the '70s. A whole generation of men and women are effectively illiterate.

At the moment, South Africa is bathing in the success of the recent elections and Nelson Mandela's unprecedented achievements. However, Mandela is 78. The goodwill he possesses will not necessarily be there for his successor, Mbeki. I cannot discern how deep the ANC's commitment is to the RDP. Politically, the ANC strikes me as being disparate and a tad undisciplined. It lacks the iron hand, authority and commitment to development of Malaysia's ruling party, UMNO. As a result, it's hard to see the RDP being put into effect by dangerous populists such as Winnie Mandela.

What is required is patience, but patience is hard to come by in the cardboard-box slums of Khayelishta and Soweto that ring the great 'white' cities. Restructuring a nation takes decades, not five years. It requires a political will that is intransigent (Lee Kuan Yew and Dr Mahathir are not consensualists) and determined. In the first five years whilst the educational foundation is being put in place, there will have to be a lot of high-profile gestures. Men such as Nthato Motlana (Mandela's former personal physician) and his publicly-listed NAIL Corporation are an indication of the growing black presence in corporate affairs. Their achievements have to be trumpeted to high heaven, farming land redistributed, roads built and unions quelled.

During all this brouhaha, a new generation must be educated – and fast – because education is South Africa's salvation. Talking to the South Africans reminded me of the importance of political expedience. There's always the need to balance the so-called immutable rights with the harsher realities on the ground. While I am not fully reconciled to the NEP myself, I understand its historical relevance and centrality to Malaysian public life.

Jakarta, Jakarta

The Sun: Ceritalah
22 July 1995

As I was crossing a footbridge over Jakarta's Jalan Thamrin last week, I stopped for a moment, high above the six lanes of traffic, and looked around me. The road (whose name changed along the way) stretched from north to south like an elephant's artery, the axis along which a city – some might say a vast kampung – had spawned.

As cars, lorries and buses roared noisily below me and pedestrians jostled me, I closed my eyes – tracing the road's triumphant path through time and space. And with each stop that I took in my imaginary journey, veering from side to side as I swerved past potholes, hand-drawn carts and Bajaj motor-rickshaws, I felt the light but insistent tap of a street-trader's hands on the windscreen as kretek cigarettes, magazines, sweets, snacks and newspapers were thrust in my face.

I began at Jakarta Kota in the north with its Dutch colonial heart – the VOC world of Jan Pieterszoon Coen, the founder of modern Batavia. Then there was Chinatown and the seedy raunchiness of Jalan Mangga Besar (whose *mangga*-like pleasures I will leave for you to figure out). After that, it was off through the stately, administrative district of Menteng with its government offices, Soekarnoesque statues and President Suharto's resplendent *istana* (Jakarta's *kraton* as it were).

Beyond Menteng and the world of the New Order, I slipped into the lanes of Tanah Abang and squeezed my way past tiny *warungs* offering *nasi unduk* and goat soup, with testicles optional for the men, before adjourning to the crowded delights of the Tanamur disco nearby. As I turned out of Tanah Abang, I passed countless forty- and fifty-storey skyscrapers, the Grand Hyatt where *ibus* wearing Gianni Versace flocked for their society lunches as their husbands siphoned off ever more cash into unnumbered Singaporean bank accounts. Then, there was the stately upper-middle-class nirvana of Kebayoran, the shopping and feeding frenzy of Blok M's *warungs*, bars and stores and onto Bogor and the hills to the south of the city.

Slipping out of my dream, I remained silent, awed by the scale of what I'd just witnessed. There was an arrogant and magnificent sweep to the city – *Ibu Kota* of a nation of close to 200 million; a forbidding impression of overwhelming size that somehow made me think of Beijing, Moscow, Delhi and Berlin – all of them cities edged with cruelty and absolutism. Suddenly the cry *'Ganyang Malaysia!'* really did seem frightening. Rooted to the spot, it was as if I had traversed the nation in microcosm, smelling the bloodied stench of its history, the naked imperialism of its leaders and the tyranny under which its downtrodden and poor had lived for centuries. Alone and in the face of such might, I was humbled.

A day later and still rather disturbed by my impressions on the footbridge, I had lunch with one of Indonesia's most prominent writers and editors – a *seniman* rather than a *wartawan*, if you like – Goenawan Mohamad, a man whose work I had long admired. Sitting alongside him, I found myself, for an instant, experiencing the same sense of awe as I'd felt the day before, high above Jalan Thamrin. Here was a man whose weekly essays (entitled *Catatan Pinggir*) in the now banned news magazine *TEMPO* were so finely written, broad and expansive that they had made me want to stop writing because of their shimmering brilliance and erudition. Here was a writer of real stature who understood the seamless connection between honesty, freedom, beauty and truth.

I was to spend much of my time in Jakarta reading and rereading his essays. Among the many, there was one essay in particular that was to leave me with a strong impression both of the country, his clear-sightedness and the differences between my world and his. The essay was called *Aku* and it dealt with Chairil Anwar's poem of the same name and the way *saya*, *aku*, *patik* and *hamba* defined the Malay sense of self.

He talked of the rugged individualism of Chairil's type of *aku* – a sense of self that rebelled against the accepted and the conventional, whether Dutch or indigenous. In the face of raw, brute power, Indonesians like Goenawan had been forced to define their sense of identity and self: firmly and rigorously. Battling against the tradition of absolutism, the individual really had to know who and what he was.

In Malaysia, by way of contrast, a much smaller and seemingly more open society had allowed the individual far greater freedoms – freedoms which we, as writers, for example, had used to tie ourselves in knots. Bourgeois conformity and ugly social pressures have reduced the plight of the individual writer to a series of nasty scuffles with the authorities.

Finally, I'd like to quote a short passage from Goenawan's essay *Mirror*: "Religion, truth, matters to do with God and man, are matters that do not have to be always related to forms and needs. 'Truth is like a God-given mirror that is now broken,' said Mohsen Makhmalbaf, the well-known Iranian film director, as quoted in the *Kompas* newspaper. Man picks up the pieces, and each person then sees his reflection in one of the pieces and thinks that he has seen the truth. The real difficulty is later, if he uses that piece of glass to stab someone who holds a different piece."

Sicklier Views, Healthier Progress

The Sun: Ceritalah

15 July 1995

Travelling around the region has taught me the importance of discarding the many prejudices I have grown up with about our neighbours. I cringe nowadays when I remember what I used to think about my Asean neighbours. If I'm honest, there was a time – not so long ago – when the three countries seemed to me, to be little more than a convenient source of domestic labour, lounge singers, charming wooden carvings, prostitutes and construction workers: good for golf trips but little else.

On a recent trip to the Philippines, I began to see the error of my 'Singaporean' ways. Firstly, I saw that my impression of the country had been distorted by the foreign media reports I had read and watched. Whilst breakfasting one morning, I came across a story in the Filipino newspapers that seemed to confirm my worst suspicions. The story concerned a sixteen-year-old Filipina maid working in the Middle East.

On June 26, 1995, the sixteen-year-old Filipina maid, called Sarah Balabagan, was sentenced to seven years imprisonment. She had been found guilty of killing her Arab employer – a man who had just raped her. The UAE court awarded her 100,000 dirhams in damages for the rape whilst fining her 150,000 dirhams for the manslaughter. The court also decided that her year-long stay in prison should be counted as part of her sentence. This meant that Sarah Balabagan, like so many others of her people, had been no more than fifteen years old when she left the Philippines to work in the UAE.

The next day, the Filipino newspapers carried an agency photograph of the girl. Sarah was slouched in her chair as she stared emptily into space. Sitting one on either side of her were the two daughters of the local Philippine ambassador. Crossing their legs like so-phisticated young ladies, they beamed radiantly for the press photographers. Looking at the photograph, I was struck by the contrast between the two – a contrast which was as stark as it was illuminating. On the one hand, there was Sarah, from Cotabato City in Mindanao – a child of poverty. On the other hand, there were Hazel and Hannah Senerez, the daughters of the Philippine Ambassador to the UAE, Roy Senerez – daughters of privilege.

It all seemed so neat – the juxtaposition of wealth and poverty and I remember smiling at my cleverness. It was only later that I saw the story in a different light.

Even before I landed at Manila airport last week, then, I knew what to expect of the Philippines: I had watched my CNN and read my *TIME* magazine. I knew I was about to arrive in the Philippines, the 'sick man of Asia'. The Philippine formula was quite simple. It was a country where a cruel and shabby dictatorship (with a penchant for shoes) had entrenched itself in a world of privilege, wealth and power – a world where the only hope for the poor was a sojourn overseas.

Visiting Manila was more in the way of confirming my preconceptions rather than anything else. I observed the keen disparity between the 'haves' and the 'have-nots' and shook my head sorrowfully. It was just as I expected. The duality of the Balabagans and the Senerezes aptly represented by the Manila Shangri-La with its rooms at RM750 a night (almost entirely full) and the cardboard-box slums lining the Pasig river. Everything was neatly arranged: rich and poor, weak and powerful.

However, after a few days, I began to suspect the neatness with which I had disposed of the Philippines. The glaring differences between the two worlds, the worlds of Balabagans and Senerezes, was only one aspect of the Philippines and I soon saw that there was great deal more to the country than rich people swinging golf clubs and Chanel handbags as they trampled all over the poor.

It was a battle to try to avoid seeing the country purely in this distorted fashion. I had been so indoctrinated with a skewered view of the place that everything else – certainly anything positive – seemed suspect. However, I knew that so long as I was so lazy in my views, my understanding of the country would be no better than the many crass CNN reports I had watched over the years.

Finally (and after a bit of a struggle), I began to see encouraging signs amidst the squalor. For example, there appeared to be a small but growing middle class – a middle class that shopped at the vast Megamall in Ortigas, bought cellular handphones, and worked for the multinationals that had invested US$1 billion in the country in the first quarter alone (much of it Malaysian). Whilst the majority of the Philippines was poor, I realised that it was important to see the country for more than its deeply entrenched social divisions. The Sarah Balabagan story was as much a reflection of national spirit as it was a tragedy.

Here was a girl from Cotabato City in Mindanao, one of eight children who had decided to travel thousands of miles in search of work. Here was a brave young woman trying to better herself and her family. While the nation had suffered from years of neglect and corruption, the spiritedness of its people and their enormous sense of hope had not entirely disappeared in the gloom.

A Bloody Beauty

The Sun: Ceritalah
12 November 1994

When I first saw Cape Town, I remember thinking to myself, this city is impossible – just impossibly beautiful. Nestled between the sea, the Table Mountain (yes, its summit is flat) and a clear, absolutely cloudless blue sky, it reminded me of Hong Kong, San Francisco and Sydney, other cities whose physical attributes had also left me short of breath.

The Cape of Good Hope – I repeated the words endlessly – buoyed up by their freshness. I had arrived in Cape Town from Johannesburg and after the sharp racial divisiveness and violent undercurrents of that city, it was a pleasure to be able to walk Cape Town's less aggressive, friendly streets.

In Jo'burg, you didn't walk anywhere. In Jo'burg, you sped from place to place in locked cars, through red lights with your eyes watching, always watching. There were too many stories of car-jackings not to watch.

Cape Town, by comparison, seemed more well-adjusted and calmer. Even the hotel, The Mount Nelson, an improbably pink confection that combined the best of The Peninsular with the Raffles, was a welcome relief. Over dinner on my first night, I watched as a large mixed race – white, black, Indian and coloured – group enjoyed dinner together. Later, when I asked who the party was for, the maitre d', a Cape Malay, told me it was for the newly appointed South African Ambassador to the US. I went to bed smiling.

My days in Cape Town were spent in a haze. I visited museums and art galleries, browsed through bookshops, watched movies, stopped at sidewalk cafes and breathed in the air, the sort of things that so-called liberal Malays like myself love to do – taking our pleasures without thinking. There were times when I thought I was in some extremely pleasant European city. It was normally just then that I was shocked out of my stupidity.

I'd spot a black stumbling through the Botanical Gardens, reeking of alcohol, lurching across the lawns and remember, 'no, I'm in Africa'. Or else I'd stumbled upon a large exhibit about Bushmen in the Natural History Museum and shudder. To the Afrikaners, the Bushmen were nothing more than animals. But somehow, that was the point: Cape Town was in Africa but somehow not 'of' Africa.

And then the doubts would begin to flow. There were times when I felt I was in two different countries, two different planes of being at the same time. On the one hand, there was the editor, Roger Vermeulen, of the black magazine *Drum*, telling me that what was once a torchbearer of the anti-apartheid movement had become a straightforward *Jelita* for black women – proof, if I needed it, that the black population was making that slow but steady progress into the middle class.

But then I'd open the newspapers and read of strikes and riots, some within a few hundred yards of the streets I had been wandering through the day before, not to mention the endless taxi-rank killings. And then there were the murders – whites killing blacks and blacks killing whites. Killings, killings, killings. After a while, it became difficult to square the gentle docility of the streets with the brutal murders I kept on reading about.

There was the story of an American exchange student called Amy Biele whose murderers were being tried whilst I was in Cape Town. She had been stuck in traffic in the township of Khayelishta. Hemmed in by cars, she had been an easy target. She was dragged from her car and beaten to death by three young blacks shouting out racist epithets. They didn't know that she was 'on their side', nor did they care. She was white and that was enough.

As if that wasn't horrible enough, there was the killing of five chicken thieves by an Afrikaner father and son. All five men were shot dead. The local police chief – and this shocked me almost as much as the killings themselves – said that there was no need to charge the two Afrikaners. They were only defending their property. The problem was that most blacks – certainly in the rural areas – had no property to speak of.

I wanted to be positive and hopeful but I found it increasingly difficult to mask my disgust. When whites asked me what it was like coming from the Third World, I stifled the anger inside me and tried to forget the ugly shanty-cities I had seen ringing the impossible beauty of Cape Town. The more I saw, somehow the more I despaired. So much blood had been shed, spilled blood which called for vengeance – "*Bloed roep om wraak*," as they said in Afrikaans and "*Siyabiza ignazi welho*," in Zulu.

It was around then that I began to realise my own anomalous situation. Though English speaking and Oxbridge educated, I was, to all intents and purposes, a 'coloured' – my father was Malay, my mother white. My parents would never have been allowed to meet, fall in love and marry in such a world. Whilst I knew that the terrible race laws were no longer in existence, I would have been one of the 'outsiders': disenfranchised and ignored.

Had I been a South African, would I have been able to forgive and forget? Could I have lived with the discrimination and not despaired? Would I have turned to violence? I don't know, nor will I ever know but the questions haunted me just as the serene beauty of the Cape had begun to sicken me with its deceptiveness and falseness. On the eve of my departure, I remembered that there was a large body of water behind the city and its gorgeous peninsula, called False Bay. The juxtaposition of the two seemed apt. Beauty and blood: hope and falseness.

Issei Sagawa

New Straits Times
30 August 1992

In the summer of 1981, a 32-year-old Japanese student called Issei Sagawa, studying at the Sorbonne in Paris, murdered a Dutch girl, Renee Hartevelt, who refused his sexual advances. He dismembered her body, eating parts of it – the breasts, which he deep-fried with mustard, the cheeks and the nose – before dividing the remains into two suitcases (the head and the limbs into one, the torso in the other) and dumping them both in the Bois du Boulogne.

Eleven years on and the self-confessed perpetrator is a magazine columnist, a best-selling novelist and sometime TV actor – in short, a celebrity trading on his past, now referred to as 'his affair' – living free, unpunished and unrepentant. I first heard of him from a friend who had interviewed him in his tiny Yokohama apartment the year before. He had told her he didn't want to talk about 'his affair', adding, however, that "I still adore the sight and shape of young Western women, particularly beautiful ones" and that she was a very attractive English woman. He added that though he was "ugly and small", he still indulged in fantasies about strong healthy bodies.

'Sagawa-kun', as he is affectionately known in the Japanese press, is still able to enjoy the company of strong healthy bodies. Living under the assumed name of Shin Nakamoto, he invites unsuspecting foreign girls back to his apartment to pose, some of them in the nude, for his oil paintings. He impresses them with his fluent French and English and plies them with cups of tea mixed with whisky, the same concoction that he gave Renee before he murdered her. Like many other people, I was astounded by the fact that he was a free man. Only then did I discover that he had been found insane and unfit for trial by the French authorities.

He was later transferred back to Japan where he was placed in a hospital. Within 15 months, he was released; the doctors no longer considered him insane. Perhaps the most extraordinary aspect of his career – and it is a career that he has carved out for himself as Japan's own 'Hannibal the Cannibal' – is the absence of moral outrage in the Japanese public at large and his remarkable celebrity.

It was with this in mind that I approached 'Sagawa-kun' for an interview. It was only after I had arranged for the interview that I realised that I had agreed to meet the man, alone and unaccompanied, at his flat at one o'clock, lunchtime.

In the days leading up to the interview, I researched the story, growing more and more unhappy with my inadvertence. With each article, each passage from his book and each transcript from his pornographic movies, I became more certain of his lunacy and certain evil.

Furthermore, he had acquired a disturbing veneer of sophistication and sobriety through his novels. His first novel *In the Fog* had been an enormous success, a best-seller. And this book had been followed up by four others, all of which dwelt upon the details of 'his affair', describing in loving detail the sensation of killing Renee, butchering her and then eating her.

The strangest twist, however, was the novel that was written about 'his affair' by one of Japan's leading literary figures and called *Letters from Mr Sagawa* which also became a best-seller. The novel went on to win the prestigious Akutagawa Prize, the equivalent of the American Pulitzer Prize. The victory was not without its criticism: three out of the seven judges disliked it. But not on moral grounds. Their objections were technical and aesthetic.

I was perplexed by the absence of moral outrage. Why weren't people disgusted with what he'd done? Why was he allowed such freedom? It's hard to imagine Jeffrey Dahmer, the American mass-murderer being able to promote himself with quite the same vigour and success. His crimes had hung like a deathly pallor over the mid-

Western city of Milwaukee, implicating the entire population for their casual disregard and callousness.

I asked one of my Japanese friends about Sagawa. She was quick to point out that she herself was horrified by the crime and that most people's interest was merely idle curiosity and no more. But this didn't satisfy me and I pressed her further. Her answer surprised me, though perhaps it shouldn't have. "The fact that the murder took place abroad makes it seem less horrifying. She was a foreigner, after all ... if she had been Japanese, it would have been very different."

The suburbs outside Tokyo are a shockingly brutal sight, an unvariegated expanse of concrete, glass and macadam that encompasses tiny homes of surprising dinginess. And because it was the height of summer, the buildings shimmered and swayed in the appalling heat. Kuala Lumpur, with its tree-lined roads, seemed a very long way away and blissfully cool by comparison.

I stepped off the commuter train at Tama Plaza, Sagawa's stop, and walked through a large air-conditioned shopping centre, past shops like Tokyu and McDonald's, reassured by the familiarity of it all. And though it was crowded with young mothers and their children dressed in bright 'Mikihouse' clothes, it was a pleasant and refreshing sight.

I could smell his flat even before I reached it. There was a thick cloud of cheap cloying deodorant (or disinfectant) hanging outside on the staircase – a scent I was to come across time and again, whenever I passed an immaculately dressed 'office lady' in the subway.

I rang the doorbell and he answered it. He was very short, 152 cm at the most and pasty-faced with pinched lips, his eyes masked by dark sunglasses. We shook hands – I don't know why – and I walked in. I slipped off my shoes and put on one of his house slippers. I chose a pair with furry rabbits on the front, thinking to myself as I did, "cannibals don't wear pink house-slippers."

Not wanting to turn my back to him, I let him show me the way (he'd shot Renee in the back and I wasn't taking chances). But as he walked in front of me, I was struck by the absurdity of my fears. He was so short and strangely built, his hips and waist large and womanly, narrowing to tiny child-like feet encased in a ridiculous pair of house-slippers. My six-year-old nephew could have beaten him up.

As I sat down, I noticed the oil paintings, bookshelves stacked with imported novels and a pencil portrait of a European girl propped up on the sofa between us, signed "With love Inge". The scent was much stronger inside the apartment, which made me wonder why he had used so much of it. Was he trying to hide something? Or was he flaunting something?

He spoke excellent unaccented English and within minutes, he was telling me about his literary influences – as if 'his affair' had been the natural culmination of some kind of artistic quest. He referred to the greats of world literature with alarming ease: Kawabata (the Japanese Nobel laureate), Tolstoy, Balzac and Shakespeare, singling out *The Tempest* and its heroine, Miranda, because of her beauty.

"I was a bookish boy," he said. "I wasn't strong and couldn't play sports. I spent my time at home reading and painting ... always Western painting. I was very influenced by Western culture. We Japanese are very Westernised. Even novelists like Kawabata are more Occidental than people care to admit. I am greatly interested in comparative literature and Western art."

He seemed determined to play the role of cultural and man-of-letters. I changed the tack and asked him what his favourite subject was to paint. He replied unhesitatingly, as if there could be any doubt. "Young, beautiful, blonde Western girls."

He said he was working on a screenplay based on another famous murder set in Japan. The incident had already been made into a film called *Ai No Corrida* (*In the Realm of the Senses*) by the director Oshima. In it, a woman and her lover experiment with various forms of increasingly violent sex. She ends up by strangling him and cutting his penis off. "I can understand what she did," he said. "People know it was done for love."

I changed the subject and asked about his acting career. "I acted the part of a Catholic priest in a show called *Alphabet 2/3*. It was an interesting experience but I found it difficult trying to memorise the lines." He didn't mention that the other players treated his past like a joke and called him 'Hannibal'. One cast member was reported as saying that if somebody was late, they joked that 'Hannibal' might have her in his fridge.

A spokeswoman for the TV production company was reported as saying that "everyone thinks Mr Sagawa should be able to come back into society, so we don't want outsiders to make this a scandalous situation." It's widely acknowledged that Sagawa is looking for a wife.

Finally I confronted him with 'his affair' and explained to him that the Malaysian public would not find it artistic or aesthetic in any way. He paused before he replied. His cheeks were a little flushed now.

"First," he said, "I am not in prison and I was never accused of anything, so I am not a criminal." He kept his eyes on my face as he spoke, daring me to disagree.

"I am hounded by the foreign press who are racist and sensationalist. My case was considered scandalous simply because I am Japanese and not European. The same thing has happened between the 'white races' but they don't speak of it."

The overpoweringly sweet scent was starting to give me a headache. I knew that he liked to speculate about whether 'his affair' was one of exquisite and pure love redeemed by art. Sickened by his story, the worrying smell and the dingy surroundings, I got up, excused myself and left. It was days before I got the scent off my clothes. Nothing in Tokyo looked quite the same after the interview. I was struck by the seeming quality of all around me.

It was as if the city was an extension of David Lynch's *Twin Peaks*, riddled with corruption, hypocrisy, barely-contained nervous tension and violence. It still seems impossible to square the serenity and beauty of the *ukiyo-e* prints that I have seen in the Tokyo National Museum with Sagawa's naked evil and the public's willing condonation … unless the order and the calm that I had witnessed everyday in the subways masked some kind of moral void. What else could explain the coexistence of the two? What else could explain Sagawa's celebrity and its basis – those descriptions of cooking and eating Renee's body … "some deliciously fatty like raw tuna, some rubbery and some fried with salt, pepper and mustard."

Oh, Kuala Lumpur ...

Men's Review
April 1995

KL, KL ... or why I love the slut that straddles the steaming rice-pot that is the Klang valley. Why, indeed? She isn't a beauty: she's no Capetown or Sydney. She isn't even a Shanghai or a New York – vast, sprawling and teeming with people like a human ant-hill. But she's mine, she's all I've got and I love her.

Which is why I always feel so cheated when I'm reminded that I was brought, squalling into the world, in Petaling Jaya, the mother of all suburbs and still the most deadening place ever invented by a Malaysian until its purgatorial hell-sister Subang Jaya was created. Bald but kicking, I was yet another of Dr Ronnie McCoy's many babies. But still I can't help wishing I'd been born in KL, maybe in Bangsar – right next to the cattle sheds, as my mother described that hospital, or the brusque metropolis that is General Hospital.

Even though I don't have KL as the *'tempat lahir'* on my IC (funny how no one calls it a KP?), KL really is my home. But why? I've spent half my life living in a country so frigid and mean that when people invite you for tea, they really do mean 'tea' and nothing else. So, why? What's with this place?

I like to think it's partly because I earned my first pay-packet on its streets, spending my cash (all RM350) on a round of drinks for the office-mates (journalists, a profession whose ability to drink at other people's expense is legendary) and a few pairs of trousers and shirts from Metrojaya. Of course, in those days (way back in 1982), Metro, as we called it then, was style, was class and was expensive: three things you wanted more than anything else in the world. Now, of course, I know better; at least I like to think I do ...

Or maybe it's because of all those nights I spent in the KL Hilton's disco, the Tin Mine, watching the mistresses of powerful, rich men playing backgammon with their toyboys. As princesses, who ought to have known better, were being violently and aggressively sick, and politicians (in an age well, well before Thamby Chik) tried hitting on your date or, failing her, her younger sister. KL then was a chocolate box where everything and everyone was possible, and in so many ways ...

Nights that were finished in a daze, chomping on *nasi lemak* in Kampung Baru whilst sitting at tables alongside the strutting *pondans* whose legs were so perfect, they inspired poetry; and fat, dowdy *mak ciks* who stirred twice as much sugar in your coffee because they were afraid you might fall asleep on your drive home ...

Years later, after a degree, a series of badly cooked dinners and a call that wasn't a telephone call, I returned to KL, ready once again, my liver hardened, my stomach iron-plated and my balls in place. I started work in the midst of a recession. Because of this, there wasn't very much work to do. Instead, guided by a man called K—, a man so expert in all things gastronomic that he was either talking about food or eating it, I spent most of my time eating and drinking. There was duck mee in Pudu; prawn mee off Jalan Silang (under the banyan tree behind Malayan Banking); *roti bakar*, kaya and the oiliest coffee at Sing Nam coffeeshop; Lafite (also known as La-kaki to the cognoscenti) when we'd been paid; and the best *nasi briyani* in the world – behind Kwong Yik Bank in the centre of the city. KL, at times, seemed to be nothing more than a succession of meals, so many meals that there were times when I realised I'd eaten breakfast, a mid-morning snack, lunch, tea, dinner and supper ...

KL, KL. If it was a succession of meals, it was also a succession of gossip – stories that floated through the air, linking everyone, high and low. From the songstress who slept with the politician who slept with the pretty TV journalist who slept with the princess who slept with the stable boy (but don't tell anybody!) who slept with the bored *mak datin* housewife who never slept with her bored Datuk husband who slept with his secretary (we men are so boring) who slept with her boyfriend who slept with his best friend who slept with the checkout girl at the supermarket in Cheras where they sell the freshest *kangkong* in KL, who slept with the gangster who slept with the call girl who slept with the record producer who slept with the songstress – and so it went on. KL, KL. I love you …

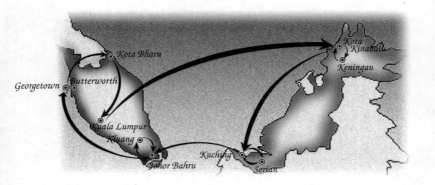

Election '95

What Is An Election?

The Sun: Ceritalah
31 December 1995

I was told by a driver (he drives a very sleek 7-series BMW) that the General Election would be held on 28 January. My electrician told me the same and he had money riding on the date. In fact, he was so certain I was tempted to place a bet as well. The driver was equally assured, telling me that his source was "best in the world. *Akupunya Datuk tahu*." When I showed some hesitation (after all, he was only a bloody driver), he said he, too, was willing to place a bet on it. However, since he was the kind of driver who hung out at the better KL hotels (better ones than I can afford), I realised his source was most likely a good deal better than anything I could come up with. It was only later that I began to question the seriousness of a society where elections were seen as betting opportunities.

It's bizarre and unfortunate but our General Elections have become something akin to a horse-race at the Turf Club with all the attendant subterfuge. Everybody I know seems to spend their days gossiping about the likely dates – the 28th, for example, is preferred because it's just before both the month of Ramadan and Chinese New Year. On the other hand, no one seems to be too bothered about what an election, in fact, really means. Despite what you may have heard from stock brokers, a General Election (I've capitalised the 'g' and the 'e' to make it stand out on the page) is not merely a buying opportunity on the KLSE.

A General Election is special, or rather, it should be special. It is not a betting opportunity. General Elections have become debased. This is because we treat them as a near irrelevance. I may be criticised for my candidness but there's no point talking rubbish. For example, the UMNO General Assembly is well known among political circles at least, to be more important than the General Election.

Anybody who says otherwise is not facing up to reality. An UMNO General Assembly decides the line-up within UMNO and as we all know, the top two figures in UMNO occupy the top two positions in Government.

So with that in mind, what is a General Election? As far as I'm concerned, a General Election is the defining moment in any democratic nation's life – it's the moment when the people, that's you and me, get to decide who rules us (at least in theory), a time when we get to evaluate and judge the relative performance of our leaders and their administration. You should always remember that our elected representatives receive their authority and status from the electorate because the electorate and the people are sovereign. We chose them – these elected representatives – entrusting them to govern fairly and responsibly. A General Election is this process writ large.

If, after acquiring power, the elected representatives are weak, corrupt or just plain useless (much, much more common), we have the duty to exercise our democratic right and elect them out of office. Being an elected representative does not mean they are there to lord it over the people. They are accountable and the election is the process whereby they are held to account.

This is all very well in a prefect world. But we do not live in a perfect world. For a start, how do we judge the performance of our elected representatives? Where do we get the information that allows us to evaluate their performance? Well, all this information comes from the Malaysian mass media which has never been over keen to publicise the failings of the Barisan Nasional, just as it has always been ready to play up the failings of the opposition.

I am not saying that we will all vote for the opposition. I don't think we will. The Government's performance has been creditable in many areas. Despite this, however, we do deserve better in terms of our General Elections. For a start, we deserve to have more information, fairer reporting and analysis. The Malaysian voting public is both responsible and practical. As such, they deserve to be treated accordingly. The coverage should be fair, impartial and open.

I want to hear what Lim Kit Siang, Tengku Razaleigh and Datuk Pairin Kitingan have to say. I am well aware of what the Prime Minister and the Deputy Prime Minister have to say on any number of issues but I'm rather ignorant on the opposition's stand on say, the Syariah, foreign investment and social issues. I may not vote for them but I want to be able to make my choice based on all the information available. In short, I want to be able to make an informed decision. By depriving me of the information, the Government is telling me that I can't be trusted to act sensibly.

Hard And Fast

The Sun: Ceritalah
8 April 1995

I am sitting down tonight to write one of the hardest columns I've
ever tried to write: a column on Datuk Seri Dr Mahathir. With the
election just around the corner, I know that I should declare what I
think about the Prime Minister and why I think it. Why is this such a
difficult thing to do? Frankly, what I have to say isn't adulatory and
we Malaysians have become so used to reading glowing reports of
everything the PM does that anything less than gushing seems sub-
versive. In many ways, this state of affairs – so typical of the Malaysia
of the '90s – is something that I deplore.

I've tried not to lie or flatter people in this column and I don't
want to start now. I want to be candid and yet I feel I can't be entirely honest without compromising myself. Discretion, then, is the
better part of valour. I am sorry for being such a coward but I hope
that you'll understand. I am neither a foreign journalist nor a hero: I
live and work in this town.

Having said that, only a fool and an idiot would deny the PM's
primary role in the Malaysian 'success story'. Credit must be given
where credit is due. The PM had the drive and the will to push the
country to where it is now – coercing agreement, at times, out of an
unwilling nation. Of course, some would say that he has been lucky.
For example, the economic slowdown of the mid-'80s was matched
by a tsunami of Japanese investment that swept across the land, spur-
ring on development. I know it's painful to recall the difficulties of
'86 and '87 – the tension and the uncertainty of those years – but we
must. Because the credit for bringing us through those years must
go to the PM, a man for whom brinkmanship has become an art.

Nonetheless, I have to be honest and admit that a lot of what I
think about the PM has been coloured by my dual experiences in

journalism and the law: two areas of Malaysian public life where the interaction with the PM has been less than happy. As a result, I have to confess that I possess a residual bitterness about the present condition of both. I'd be lying if I said otherwise and as I said earlier, I don't want to lie.

The events of the past few years have moderated the bitterness. Despite this, instead of becoming clearer, my views have become more complicated and almost contradictory. Much of this has to do with the fact that the PM – a man who has been in power for well over 14 years – has, deliberately or not, shaped my life and my way of thinking. Malaysian political life for anyone in his or her early thirties is Datuk Seri Dr Mahathir. As such, what he thinks and how he thinks has permeated the fabric of society, colouring it much like a dye, until the society resembles him. I confess that I have been coloured and swayed in the same way. I, Karim Raslan – a product of the Western liberal humanist tradition, of Cambridge University, the Inns of Court, a world of unfettered human rights and press freedoms – confessing that my world view has changed? Is that possible? Yes, it most definitely is. And to be frank, much of the reason for this change is due to the PM. How?

Frankly, I have grown to see the governance of Malaysia in terms of 'ends', rather than 'means'. I understand now that in ruling our country, 'the hands cannot be too soft' – there have to be times when the interests of the nation as a whole have to ride roughshod over the rights of individuals. I look at all the positive attributes of what the PM (and his team) have achieved because I feel that these things – the large middle class, a growing sense of national identity, the infrastructure sprouting up around us and the extraordinary prosperity – could not have been attained without sacrificing the 'Western' ideals of freedom of speech, association and, at times, even the rule of law. As I said 'the hands cannot be too soft': ominous but true.

I know the so-called 'Asian' model of development that the PM espouses is a hotly contested subject but I look around me and I see the fruits of this alternative way – I see the prosperity and the stability. I compare it, for example, with South Africa, a country I have visited regularly. The South Africans seem determined to follow the 'Western' model, with its litany of rights and freedoms. I worry for them. How, I wonder, can they tackle their skewered, shattered economy and uplift their impoverished black majority unless they, like our PM back in the mid-'80s, dispense with the freedoms that I was taught to cherish so dearly.

Datuk Seri Dr Mahathir's tenure as Prime Minister has seen a sea-change in Malaysia: a change that encompasses highways, airports, factories and schools as much as it does the mindsets of those who man these buildings, institutions and installations. I recognise the nation's debt to him but end by asking whether the same pattern of policies can necessarily see us into the new millennia with quite the same success.

'Virtual' Election Underway

The Sun

14 April 1995

Along with my weekly column, I shall also be providing you with an almost daily 'take' on the elections. Starting in KL, I shall be crossing the South China Sea to Sabah, travelling down to Sarawak and then back again to Johor, Penang and Kelantan, all within the next ten days: *insha'allah* and MAS willing.

However, I won't be giving you the who's, when's and what's but the how's and why's – an impression of the places I'll be passing through, the people I meet and the worlds they inhabit: a personal, quixotic state of the nation.

But before I start on my odyssey – my *rantau* – I should first say that the modern-day election isn't just about *ceramahs*, public meetings, canvassing and the like. True, they all still exist. I know everyone loves on opposition *ceramah*. They're the hottest because they *hantam* all the cabinet ministers in turn. However, I suspect, they're a nostalgic throwback to the days of the Tunku, Dato' Onn and Tun Tan and that many people miss the camaraderie and fun of it all.

Preserved in the idea of the *ceramah* is the romantic memory of Malaysia as a small, manageable polity (a large kampung) where everybody knows one another: charming but outmoded. Why? Because the modern-day election is fast becoming an electronic one.

The election is broadcast 'live' to your homes in TV news bulletins and delivered hot off the press to your doorsteps every morning. The mass media has pulled the election into our homes. The (albeit one-sided) contests are waged on the TV screens and in the newspapers as the *ceramah* for 500 has been replaced in importance by the evening news for five million. As electronic communications grow ever more accessible, their reach will continue to mushroom until such time as the *ceramah* itself is conducted over Internet. Just imagine, for example, Mohamad Sabu on Internet – at least he'd be able to interface to his heart's content with the female PAS party-workers without having to worry about *khalwat*.

So how has this affected the 1995 elections? I think it means that a 'virtual' election has been underway – an election quite separate from the official one but just as important, if not more so.

In the weeks just prior to the declaration of the election, I'd been plagued by the sneaking suspicion that the polls had already been declared, that the race had begun but that no one had thought to inform the electorate. The torrent of patriotic songs on TV, the outpouring of good news everywhere else (a boom in *ciku* production in Ulu Ketiak Baru) and the beaming face of our charming Information Minister was beginning to 'get' to me.

Now, I'm as patriotic as the next man and I like my *Sejahtera Malaysia* at the end of transmission on TV2, but there comes a point when enough is enough. Negotiating the 'virtual' election is a bizarre experience and one that takes you through treacherous undercurrents. Although the campaigning period is meant to last for only ten days, the 'virtual' election has been going on since the beginning of the year. Besides that, the 'virtual' election has dictated the terms of the real, actual election, providing the electorate with a set of arguments that are hermetic and self-contained. Put quite simply, the 'virtual' election says the BN has ruled so well over the past four years that they should be returned to power again. Full stop.

There is little room for other voices, dissent or debate: the 'virtual' election has smothered all of that in patriotic songs.

So, as I pack my bags in anticipation of my journey, I wonder whether I'm wasting any time. Shouldn't I be spending the next ten days in front of a TV, surrounded by newspapers? Isn't the world of the 'virtual' election more real and more important? I can't answer the question now. However, it's partly in search of the answer to that question that I am taking to the road. In a way, I hope I'm proven wrong. I hope the election still belongs to the people.

Changing The Fabric

The Sun: Ceritalah
15 April 1995

Last week, as a prelude to the election, I wrote about the Prime Minister and what I thought about him, his record, his strengths and his weaknesses. I hoped that my assessment would be of some use to the readers, if only as a kind of sounding board, something that would stimulate debate. In that respect, I was proved all too correct, though in a way that I was to find initially disheartening and yet ultimately rewarding.

How was it rewarding? Well, the reappraisal of his tenure showed me that whilst the economy had grown magnificently, our political life had not. It was as if the LRT now being laid through the heart of KL was expected to run on rotten belian wood railway sleepers. But before I discuss that, let me tell you about the immediate response to the column.

As soon as the issue hit the streets, I was inundated by personal complaints. However, they weren't complaining about my criticisms of the PM. Far from it – they were laughing at what I had to say! Laughing at what they said was my feebleness and the irrelevance of my arguments. One friend even took me aside and complained to me about what he called my 'whitewashing' of the Mahathir years – about my self-censorship and my cowardliness.

"Hey," he asked me, "are you trying to get some federal contract because if you are, you're making a damn fool of yourself, you know? Call yourself impartial? *Ampu ampu* only: you're just another toady." Embarrassed by the criticism and my friend's inferences, I decided to reread my column.

Scanning it once again, I must confess that many of his criticisms were correct. I had been too charitable about the PM's tenure to date: praising the achievements whilst skating over the weaknesses and failures. I hadn't mentioned the centralising of power and influence, the cronyism, our deteriorating environment, the lack of accountability, the complacency and corruption of many of those in public life, nor the poverty of public debate – a list of woes that was almost as sizeable as the achievements. To my horror and self-disgust, I realised that I was in danger of becoming one of those grovelling journalists and public apologists we all talk to, smile at and yet despise.

Why was I so concerned about this? Let me explain. It's rather as if a banker has been told that his bank is neither credit-worthy nor secure from robbery. For a writer then, his credibility strikes at the heart of why he writes and what he writes just as much as a banker's credit-worthiness lies at the heart of a banker's *modus vivendi*. An insolvent, improperly defended bank is not a bank. It's just a pile of money waiting to be appropriated. Similarly, a column or essay without honesty or credibility is nothing more than a random collection of words.

And yet despite all this, despite the possibility of sounding like a stooge and at the risk of losing the little credibility that I possess, I know that my instincts, in the main, lie with the PM and his government. I may criticise but that does not mean that I don't subscribe to the 'whole', as it were.

Nonetheless, I admit that I had lacked balance when discussing the PM's tenure. However, I feel I've rectified that failing, and having rectified it, I am still of the opinion that the woes I've just listed above have been more than compensated for by their attendant benefits. Politics is lived and played out in the real world, a world where sacrifices do have to be made and hard decisions taken – decisions that will often displease a large section of the population even though they will (or should I say 'may'), at the end of the day, bring benefits to the same people.

The more I thought about Dr Mahathir's record, the more I realised that it was important that these elections should mark a transition that was long overdue, in both the nature and style of governance. What had been necessary for the mid-'80s – the years of economic upheaval and political strain – was now no longer required. A property-owning middle class, that bulwark of stability, has been created in the past decade. With this class happily installed in the endless Tamans of Puchong, Seberang Perai, Penampang and Pelangi, the spectre of mass violence and racial strife has been dispelled.

Quite simply, the Malaysian paradigm has changed. Our political life no longer matches our robust economy. It is stunted by comparison – fixated by race, an excessive rural imbalance (to the detriment of the more progressive urban voters), a subsidy mentality based on handouts, political patronage and narrow-mindedness. These things are not irrelevant. They will hamper our continuing development unless they are tackled soon.

While it is important to acknowledge the achievements of the past, it is the remaining problems that should be addressed more squarely. And, to my mind, our political life must be allowed to grow to match the changing times. Malaysia is turning into a middle-class nation with middle-class concerns: accountability, pollution, education, technological innovation, transparency of government, greater press freedoms and corruption. It is these issues that will dominate the political arena in years to come. Now is the time to start addressing them.

Orang KL And Their Political Sentiments

The Sun

16 April 1995

"Politics," Ghazali (all the names have been changed) said, his eyes fixed on mine, "is all about winning and about getting on the winning side. Anything else is for fools and I am not a fool."

He turned away from me and took a neat sip from his beer, leaving me to think about his words. We had just eaten one of those unsatisfying Italian meals – noodles and sauce for RM20 that seem such a rip-off when you know you can get *char kway teow* for one-tenth the price just around the corner.

I wasn't entirely prepared for his cynicism and scorn. Sitting in silence, I wondered whether I was being unduly naive setting off on the election trail. Was I missing the point, or was he? Looking out of the large windows, I caught sight of the gleaming BMWs, the Range Rovers and the Mercedeses nestled in the car-park – the trophies of the NEP and a decade of staggering economic growth. A piercing and, at times, almost jarring voice – 1 think it was Ning Baizura's – scorched the air in the arctic-cold bar.

"I don't care about the elections," he added aggressively. "It's either a 'buy' or a 'sell' opportunity, depending on how you see it and I think it's a 'sell'. Hey, politics is about self-interest! Don't give me the bull about serving the community. *Aku tahu* only too well."

But before he could continue, Juriah, a lady banker, interrupted.

"Don't get moral with us, Karim. I can't stand that – not while I'm eating Italian, please? Principles are all very well in your columns. But this is real life, now. The election results are a foregone conclusion and I'm not going to waste my time talking about them."

Laughing, she added: "I've come out tonight to escape the TV and the newspapers. I'm only bothered about who are going to be the new players. Now, that's really important."

As she said the fateful word 'player', everyone around the table fell silent. This was important and somebody piped up: "I want to know who's going to be the next MB of Johor."

"Where's Muhyiddin going to be posted to in the Federal Government? Who's replacing Ibrahim Saad in Penang if he moves to KL? And the new faces – like Zahid Hamidi, Mustapha Mohamed, Kamal Salleh and Nazri Aziz, where will they be? Now that's important."

Everyone nodded. This was serious and every one of them needed to concentrate – myself included. As the talk swirled from one politician to another, from state to state (settling on Kelantan only briefly because as Juriah said – "Kelantan! Who cares? If they want to live in poverty, that's their problem"), I began to sense an underlying feeling of resentment from all around the table.

It was as if the process, the entire political process – the parties, the nominations and the elections themselves – didn't belong to any of us. We were the 'orang KL'. KL was our kampung and yet despite its affluence and veneer of power, we were excluded from the game. We were merely observers.

Driving home later, as my car juddered over the potholes and veered past the Bangladeshi workers retarring the road, I tried to think why my friends and I should feel so separate and apart from what was going on – from the furore that would grip the nation for the next ten days. Was it possible that we were disenfranchised? The thought struck me as ludicrous and I almost laughed.

However, I suddenly recalled meeting an Umno politician after the 1990 election who had shaken his head mournfully as he discussed the urban Malay vote. According to him, many of the urban Malays had forsaken Umno. It wasn't as if they'd voted DAP or PAS. No, most of them had just given up on the political process. They had what they wanted: jobs, homes, cars and education for the children. Politics, these people seemed to feel, was for those who didn't have the 'goodies' of development.

At the time, I had thought the politician was crazy. The BN had just won the 1990 elections. What more did he expect? Now, however, I understood.

These friends of mine were all bright, well-educated and rich. And, like me, they were beneficiaries of the NEP. However, the political world was alien to them, something rural, grubby and distasteful – *tak cukup style-lah*: a world their parents knew. It was not their own world, however.

We had all become 'orang KL', living our lives according to the customs of the city. We had lost touch with our rural roots (the world of our parents and grandparents), the same roots that nurtured Umno over the decades. What we had failed to see was that the party would continue to voice the aspirations of the rural constituencies to the exclusion of the urban Malays until such time as people like my friends at the bar actually took part in the political process.

Pallid And Boring Compared To Keningau

The Sun

17 April 1995

Two-and-a-half hours from Kota Kinabalu, along a road so sheer and perilous that it is swathed in mist for much of the day (when it isn't being swept away by rain, that is), there happens to be a factory so large and modern that the company operating it, Aokam Perdana, has became the toast of the Southeast Asian stockbroking community – not to mention the largest KFC I've ever seen outside KL.

The same town, Keningau, was almost inaccessible as recently as 15 years ago – a thought which now seems inconceivable.

Keningau is tucked away in what is said to be the Kadazan-Dusun heartland. The town is set in a broad plain, dotted with massive bamboo groves. The plain is itself sheltered from the coast by the jagged peaks and perpendicular valleys of the Crocker Range.

Despite its past isolation, Keningau is, in fact, a minor crossroads of sorts. One can head south to Tenom, Nabawan and Indonesian Kalimantan – Murut country – or north to Tambunan and Mount Kinabalu: either way dotted with small, farming communities, where the air is so cold and damp in the morning, you wish you'd never gotten up.

I thought it would be the ideal place to begin my trek across Malaysia. 'Ulu' and sheltered, it appealed to my romantic sense of things. Well, I got that completely wrong because Keningau was a yelping boomtown – Wild West but gone East and Kadazan. Pakistani cloth-sellers in *shalwar kameez*, slick Rayban-wearing *towkays* in open-topped Cherokee Wranglers, Timorese labourers, Toraja farmers from the mountains of Sulawesi, more four-wheel drives than you've had hot dinners, Bugis men (who you wouldn't want to have as your ancestors), urchins selling cigarettes by the stick, courting couples waiting to see the film *Penyu* (and those who had survived it), girls with *tudungs* fluttering behind their heads and the hoarse but sensual wailing of the Ratu Rock, Ella, pouring out of the mini-compo behind me. Oh yes, and I was there, too, scribbling away like mad whilst sipping the oiliest *kopi-o* ever.

On a sweltering nomination day morning, I was there waiting for the arrival of the Huguan Siou, or Paramount Chief, Datuk Joseph Pairin Kitingan, president of PBS and the incumbent MP. While Pairin's candidacy was the initial reason for my visit, I soon realised that neither he nor elections were as engrossing as this strange little boomtown in the heart of Borneo.

I know this upsets all the laws of journalism but quite frankly I didn't care because that morning, Pairin's decade-long tussle with the Barisan National and the Barisan's tussle with him seemed pallid and uninteresting compared to the town he represented in the Dewan Rakyat.

However, in a fitful attempt to be the dutiful journalist, I watched the amiable crowd at the town's sports ground as they grouped and regrouped, awaiting the nominations. From where I was standing on the grandstand, the figures looked rather like blood cells under a microscope – moving from the Barisan encampment (blue cells) to the PBS (red, white and blue) and then back again. However, another set of cells – a group of sportswomen (pink and healthy) – seemed to be functioning quite happily without recourse to either of the larger groupings. I don't know why but it made me think of a Health Ministry anti-AIDS campaign crossed with Rakan Muda.

But back to the sportswomen. There were two groups of them: the first was preoccupied with the high jump and the intricacies of the Fosbury flop; the second was composed of stern-faced girls leaping over hurdles and one solitary figure who was sprinting the 100 m whilst tied to a large car tyre. I was struck by her determination and observed silently.

Meanwhile, the two groups of supporters (Barisan and PBS) had gathered on different sides of the *padang*: the PBS, loud and exuberant; the Barisan, more subdued and dignified. The Barisan group moved across to the running track as if they were completing a victory lap. I shook my head. Given Pairin's rock-solid majority, the gesture seemed premature.

In the rush that ensued, I dashed forward and asked each of the candidates (the Barisan candidate was a dazed-looking, youngish former state sprinter called Ellron Albert Angin who, it was said, ran faster than the wind) whether or not they were going to win.

Having received their not-unexpected answers – they were both going to win – I left the sports ground and headed back to the town. Maybe it was just me, but the entire political process seemed lack-lustre and tedious. Sabah, I realised, had seen too many elections in too few years: too much politicking and not enough straightforward living of life. All the posturing on the sports ground: the songs, the taunts and the 'frog' jokes seemed flat and contrived compared to the raucousness of the town, the plaintive lilt of the Ratu Rock, Ella and the quiet determination of that girl tugging at the rubber tyre.

Sabah Calls For A Different Tune

The Sun
18 April 1995

West Malaysians like me who arrive in Kota Kinabalu are easily deceived by Sabah. There are so many superficial similarities, we tend to forget the two and half hours it's taken to fly there and the passport controls on arrival.

We step out of Kota Kinabalu airport, only to discover that everything is very much the same as in the peninsula: the street-signs are in Bahasa and there are Protons parked alongside the local Maybank. However, at least in my case, the bank happened to be closed for Good Friday. Good Friday? Yes, Good Friday because the state has a substantial Christian population.

Those two and a half hours (Jakarta, Bangkok and Ho Chi Minh City are closer to KL) make a vast difference, infusing the state with a personality that is raunchier, rougher and more straightforward. Similarly, Sabah has its own points of reference, its own history, myths and heroes whose exploits are emblazoned in the broadsheet pages of *The Daily Express* or the tabloid *Borneo Mail*.

For example, Matlan Marjan, the pint-size Sabah footballer and striker will mean nothing to a KL-ite. But to a Sabahan, the Bajau footballer who led the state to its recent Malaysia Cup victory is a demigod – albeit a short one. Almost single-handedly, he gave Sabahans something to be proud about.

As one young sales executive said to me over a drink, "We've had nearly ten years of political disruption here in Sabah, blackouts, brownouts, illegals, crime and squalor – you name it, we've had it. I can't tell how much of a relief it is to have something like the Malaysia Cup to get excited about. Something that's clean and unconnected with bribery. Something that has nothing to do with politics. I'm sick of politics and elections. We seem to have an election every year!"

I had touched a sensitive point and he continued without being prompted. "In fact, Sabah would be a whole lot better off if we put all our politicians on a ship and set them adrift in the South China Sea. You could say I'm suffering from election fatigue."

Being cynical about politicians is common the world over. In Sabah, however, the distaste for the political class exceeds anything you will find in the Semenanjung. In many ways, the contempt is deserved, especially after the undignified bout of party-hopping that followed last year's state elections. Let me give you an example.

A lawyer told me a joke about a Sabah politician who had a frog stuck on his head. The politician, troubled by the frog who would not leave, decided to go and see a doctor. As soon as he walked into the consulting room, the frog piped up. "Doctor, doctor, can you get this wart off my buttocks?" I rest my case.

Nonetheless, this should not obscure the fact that Sabahans have their own culture, *adat* and languages. Driving through the Kadazan areas of Penampang, these differences can be quite striking: churches enisled by padi fields, wild dogs and pigs, not to mention the election placards in Kadazan – a language which reminded me of German because of its astoundingly long words.

The Muslim areas are different as well. The Bajau fishing villages outside Tuaran do not look or feel like fishing villages in Terengganu. Being a Muslim in Sabah doesn't necessarily mean that you are culturally Malay. *Masuk Islam* does not immediately equate with *Masuk Melayu*.

I've met Bajau Muslims, Visayan Muslims, Murut Muslims, Kadazan Muslims and Rungus Muslims: many of whom speak their own language as well as Bahasa. These people are not carbon copies of people in KL. Nor do they want to be carbon copies either. To deny the difference then is to defy fate, history and geography: in short, a very foolish thing to do. And it was, in many ways, because everybody denied these kind of differences in the '80s that federal-state relations deteriorated so badly.

An example of the touchiness over federal-state ties is the way we in West Malaysia tend to say "Sabah joined Malaysia in 1963." One retired Sabahan civil servant corrected me on this.

"That's rubbish. We formed Malaysia with the Federation, Singapore and Sarawak. This doesn't mean that I don't believe in Malaysia. I do. All I'm saying is that we have to be treated according to terms of that agreement. Nothing more and nothing less."

Hitherto, we peninsular Malaysians have tended to see such an argument as being almost treasonable. What we have failed to understand is that the agreement was based on a great deal of common sense – common sense that didn't try to smooth over the very real differences that do exist.

Driving through KK for the past few days has taught me one thing and that is the urgent need for Umno Sabah, for example, to develop a personality that is in keeping with the culture and *adat* of its members here in Sabah. Obviously, this culture shouldn't be too divergent from the party's base in West Malaysia. Having done that, the party has to try to wean the political debate off the cul-de-sac of federal-state relations and onto the familiar track of development politics.

A Disconcerting Kind Of Hush

The Sun
20 April 1995

Kuching was as hushed and calm as Kota Kinabalu had been chaotic
and disorderly. The election seemed a long, long way away. But there
again nobody in their right mind would ever have accused Kuching
of being a buzzing metropolis at any time of the year.

As soon as I arrived in Kuching, I looked out for campaign posters and streamers but I couldn't seem to see any which surprised
me because I knew that the town, quite unlike the rest of the state,
was a DAP stronghold and I expected to see the DAP incumbent
Sim Kwang Yang's face pasted everywhere. The rocket, however,
was more conspicuous by its absence – smothered by the *dacing*
and ambition of the Barisan candidate Song Swee Guan, who also
happened to be both the mayor of Kuching Selatan as well as a local
state assemblyman (the Barisan was obviously economising in terms
of manpower).

Having hunted throughout the predominantly-Chinese areas of
Bintawa and Pending for DAP posters, I resigned myself to failure.
Was it simply a case, I wondered, of "Desperately Seeking Sim",
perhaps?

Then again, no one appeared too keen to show their support for
him. This perplexed me. Why was his public presence (he was the
incumbent, after all) so muted? Were the people too afraid to hang
out his posters? Too lazy? Too poor? I never found out the answer
but it worried my sense of fair play, just as other aspects of the town,
which, at times, seemed more like a stage set for *The Stepford Wives*,
replete with ever-smiling but lobotomised housewives, troubled me.

However, I had to confess that despite its disconcerting undercurrents, Kuching was a charming town. It was clean, well-mannered
and rich – the apogee of middle-class Malaysia and a bourgeois para-

dise; full of parks, public spaces, good schools and pleasant shopping areas. However, the town's wealth was a little surprising when I realised that its real business was the business of governance. Sarawak, at least to my mind, was an example of one man's determination to lead from the front, as well as the positive and negative aspects of almost complete political control.

As one lawyer said to me: "Power, real power and patronage lies at the state level. The federal election is irrelevant.

"The candidate," he added, "with the better machinery wins. Sarawak is very simple."

Remembering the titanic struggle of Tun Rahman Yaakob and his nephew, the present Chief Minister, I nodded knowingly. Even I knew that the federal elections didn't bring with them the control of Sarawak's forest wealth.

Although the lawyer disdained the federal elections, Sarawak's Barisan machinery had achieved an enviable result, returning nine MPs unopposed. It was as if the Barisan's much-vaunted machinery in Sarawak had achieved its logical and expected end: an election where voters had been relegated into the position of onlookers, cheering on a process from which they were now redundant.

It was partly because of this unease that I arranged to visit the predominantly-Bidayuh constituency of Serian. I was there to meet a man called Raymond Daling, a worker in the Barisan machinery (a cog in the wheel as it were) who was to show me around the constituency. His name gave me no end of pleasure as I repeated it over and over again in the car.

"Hello, Raymond, Daling," I said to myself before deciding that the pause between the Raymond and the Daling might be misconstrued as an advance of sorts and that I should say "Hello Raymonddaling" in one breath.

Unfortunately, Raymond (Daling or not) was not to be found in the Barisan Bilik Gerakan, a shophouse that buzzed purposefully and I was left to my own devices.

Driving around Serian, I noted that the town had been honoured with its very own bypass – a reflection, I thought, of a sense of civic self-importance that rather outweighed reality. Driving around aimlessly – somebody had to use the bypass – I saw a group of party workers erecting a rickety, uneven poster on the massive roundabout outside the town.

The lettering was crude and the poster home-made, but the men were engrossed in setting it up. Attracted by the spectacle, I stopped and chatted with them.

To my surprise, the poster was for an independent candidate called Dr Eric Marcel Munjan, who I later found out to be an X-ray specialist from a private hospital in Kuching. Here, at last, I had discovered a whiff of what I'd been looking for and I dashed off to meet the man himself. He was gray-haired and though standing as an independent, he was a member of one of Barisan's constituent parties, SNAP. Most of the Sarawakian parties had a slightly surreal onomatopoeic ring – witness the various SNAPs and the SUPPs.

His Bilik Gerakan was a mess. There seemed to be little in the way of organisation – just a lot of enthusiasm. He explained his reasons for standing and his principles, whilst his supporters milled around. He was quiet, understated and convincing: this, I thought with relief, was politics of the heart. This was the antidote to all that garbled nonsense about machinery and processes. Having said that, I was torn by a dilemma. Was it possible, I wondered, to have the order and prosperity of Kuching without the political control? Whilst I rather despised the town's slow, tranquil ways, I knew that most of its inhabitants preferred its stability to Kota Kinabalu's more raucous political life.

Was Eric Manjun's impassioned plea for justice, in fact, unwittingly a prelude to the kind of chaos that typified the political landscape of Sabah? Was freedom of choice, one freedom too many?

New Bold Dream

The Sun
21 April 1995

If Penang, Kelantan and Sabah are the extremities of what constitutes Malaysia – both politically and geographically – Johor and Johor Bahru must be close to the centre. And, more important than being just its centre, JB is also the spiritual home of Umno, the site of its formation and the hometown of its first great leader, Datuk Onn Jaafar.

I had come to JB, midway through my election round, to find out how the heartland of Umno was adjusting to the new paradigms. I hadn't come to determine what the election result would be. That was immaterial. I knew, just as everybody else knew, that the election result was a foregone conclusion. I was interested in the future of the party, the party that had ruled our lives for so many years, and whether or not the '95 elections had suggested where it was headed.

As the plane touched ground at JB's Senai airport, after days in East Malaysia, I knew I'd returned to a more familiar landscape because try as I might, Sarawak and Sabah were still foreign territory. They were states where I had been forced to think before I spoke, qualifying everything I said because I couldn't afford to take anything at face value. Things which I took for granted in the peninsula were opaque or contradictory on the other side of the South China Sea.

Nonetheless, I'd chosen the Barisan redoubt of Johor as my testing point – in part because JB lies at the heart of the Umno myth of creation and I wanted to see how that myth had developed over the generations. Had the schism that produced Semangat 46 really destroyed the soul of the party? Or was the party, in fact, changing in ways that very few of us had noticed?

In one respect, I was fortunate because, in a previous guise and many years before, I'd worked with Datuk Onn's grandson,

Hishammuddin. In those days, he was just a young lawyer with a gold-plated pedigree. However, I'd be lying if I didn't say that Hisham was always slightly different. I know 'good breeding' and *berbudi bahasa* are old-fashioned expressions but they're the best way of pin-pointing the special qualities he seemed to possess.

But I'm a sceptic at heart and I've always found his transition from KL boy to Johor boy a little ingenuous, even forced. And it was in search of the truth about this sea-change, not to mention the skein history that linked him to his grandfather – the man who wanted to open Umno to all Malaysians – that made me stop over in Johor and Tenggara, the parliamentary constituency where Hisham was standing.

Looking at the map before I visited him, I saw that Tenggara was a strange, stretched-out constituency that reached from Kluang in the north to Kota Tinggi in the south. In between, it was predomi-nantly agricultural with vast oil palm plantations, some of which were Felda settlements. In the Bilik Gerakan of the Gunung Lambak State Assembly seat (one of the two state seats within the parliamentary seat of Tenggara), I saw the patchwork of areas: some Chinese, such as Kampung Yap Tau Sar where I was at the time, and others, such as Felda Tongkat, which were almost exclusively Malay – but Malays of Javanese descent.

Interestingly, the Bilik Gerakan itself stood on a patch of ground that divided Kampung Yap Tau Sar into two. On one side of the muddy *padang*, there were Chinese houses with their distinctive red altars and joss sticks; on the other, the Malay houses, festooned with bougainvillea and orchids. Since I was early, I popped into a small stall run out of the living-room in a house on the Chinese side of the divide, leaping from one world to another.

And it was this racial division that also concerned me now. Would the leaders of Hisham's generation – the 'thirtysomethings' – be able to pull together the disparate parts that go to make up our country? I had watched him campaigning in the Felda settlement of Sri Bayu, where with his fellow candidates at state level, the loquacious Asmaon Ismail and the very attractive former schoolteacher Halimah Mohamed Sadique. The three of them had 'staged' a *ceramah* which was halfway to a rock concert. Clearly the three of them (they were all under 40) had the charisma and the charm. I dubbed them the 'Dream Team' and smiled as they bantered with the crowd like an Imuda or Ahmad Busu.

Later that night, they addressed a more sombre crowd of *pak ciks* in *kain pelekats*, demure *mak ciks* in matching *bajus* as well as kids who were more concerned about picking their noses and playing in the mud. Then, as Hisham spoke, I saw that he noticed a group of Chinese men sitting to the side. They had looked a bit uncomfortable but he stretched his arm out and started talking about a "one Malaysian people: *Melayu ren*, *Cina ren*, *India ren* and *Kadazan ren*." It went over the heads of most of the audience. But for that one brief moment, I had a premonition and a hope that we were ready for this leap into the future.

Kit Siang's Dream Fraught With Dangers

The Sun

21 April 1995

Lim Kit Siang arrived after 10. A small, frantically bobbing flag with the DAP's rocket preceded him. The rocket seemed to shake and dance like a lion on the first day of Chinese New Year. A sinuous ripple of acknowledgment coursed through the crowd of 4,000. I watched as the heads at the front of the audience, like the scales of a large dragon, turned away from the outdoor video screens, in search of Kit Siang. The tension suddenly was electric.

From my perch on the open landing of the Fortuna restaurant (high above the crowd) where the DAP leader was scheduled to give his evening speech, I could see the hands stretching out to greet him, his white short-sleeved shirt and the handlers who accompanied him.

I had been observing the almost exclusively Chinese audience as they, wide-eyed and open-mouthed, listened to the speakers. Clad in shorts, slippers and T-shirts and riding mopeds, they were the kind of people that I, as a middle-class KL-ite, never noticed. It was as if a veil had been lifted from my eyes. All at once, a people I'd thought nothing of – nothing at all – had materialised right in front of me. Thousands of them. They looked like stallholders, car mechanics, shop assistants, clerks and contractors. And, for the first time in many years, I felt I was the outsider.

Reading the DAP leaflets in Chinese, they nodded and laughed at the stream of Hokkien and Mandarin dialects that I knew nothing of. Suddenly, the speaker paused. Instead of words, music flowed through the loudspeaker system – a stirring song with a martial beat that made my hair stand on end. As Kit Siang approached the steps that led up to the restaurant, he turned around and greeted the crowd. There were cheers, applause and more music – a deep-throated roar from the dragon. Turning his back to the crowd, he strode inside. I asked a fellow journalist what the words of the song meant. He answered somewhat enigmatically, "If you win, you must fight".

I had been waiting for Kit Siang for well over two hours. Finally, here was the 'demon' himself, the man my Government had labelled a chauvinist – 'the CM with power'. Here he was in the flesh. He had been the object of so much vilification both before the election and during it, that I knew I had to see him speak in person. Would I be comfortable being ruled by him? That was the simple question I had set myself.

Though only 54 years old, I had the impression that this election was to be his swan song, his last attempt at seizing the ultimate: real political power. We have all heard his criticisms of the Barisan government. Suffice to say there were many points on which I could not help but agree with him – certainly when it came to the issues of corruption, press freedom and human rights. Agree but disagree, because as I've said time and again, this nation of ours does not live in the ideal world. Malaysia cannot withstand the full onslaught of all these 'rights'.

His voice was grating but authoritative as he switched effortlessly from Malay, to English, to Hokkien and to Mandarin. He hit out at the media's coverage of him. His main point, however, seemed to lie with 'the CM with power' argument, an argument that I, for one, could not agree with. Wasn't it Kit Siang himself who'd demolished the one Chinese leader with 'real' stature – Tun Dr Lim Chong Eu – back in the 1990 polls? Hadn't he, in fact, done a terrible disservice to his own community?

Tun Lim's power and authority had been real. But it had been acquired over decades, not overnight. He had fended off the incursions of the federal government and Umno in a manner that was not confrontational. Without the colossus and his 20 years of experience, Penang's political structure was bound to change and change it did.

There was no doubt in my mind that Kit Siang was a worthy opponent: shrewd and formidable. The DAP's inclusion of Malay candidates has been a master stroke. Nonetheless, his obsession with Penang, his fixation on seizing power had led him to destroy the equilibrium that had once prevailed in the island. Wasn't he, I thought, in danger of repeating the same scenario, weakening forever, perhaps, the Chinese control of Penang?

The Numbers Game As It Is Played In Perai

The Sun
22 April 1995

As Rani Ibrahim, the Deputy Prime Minister's elder brother took to the rostrum, a light titter of expectation shivered through the audience of middle-aged, *tudung*-wearing *mak ciks*. With every slightly risque joke, they laughed: coy and yet flirtatious.

However, it was a wonder they could even hear his broad Penang intonation because the road alongside the *ceramah* throbbed with the ugly groans of heavy lorries making their way to the container port of Butterworth. Here, in Bagan Dalam, a kampung cheek-by-jowl with the northern region's premier port, the democratic process, like the TV show *Pi Mai Pi Mai Tang Tu*, had to be conducted at full volume.

Apart from the lorries, there were the more familiar sounds of water being boiled, tea urns filled, and cups and saucers clinking in the background. There was so much noise from the kitchens that I began to suspect that the ladies involved in the catering thought the crowd outside was merely waiting to test their *mee goreng istimewa* and *teh susu* – "Elections? Hah! Who cares? Try my pandan sponge cake?"

Catching sight of the lady in charge, I could see she was as convinced of her calling as Lim Kit Siang or the PM. She would feed and water the Umno faithful if it killed her. I had no doubt that if Datuk Seri Dr Mahathir had been there, she would have sat him down and given him a cup of tea and a curry puff. Nobody escaped her attention and I felt sure that Dr K. Rajapathy, the BN candidate with the Tamil movie star smile, would have been subjected to her culinary creations – chocolate pandan cake and *mee rebus* a la *Wanita* magazine.

Despite the air of relative calm, the jokes and the back-slapping, I could tell I was among the Umno faithful, people for whom politics meant *masuk Umno*. Nonetheless, the battle in the state seat of Perai (of which Bagan Dalam is a small ward) is a tough one.

Glancing at a notice-board behind my head, I noticed a torrent of numbers. Numbers jumbled up with names, percentages, totals and subtotals that made no sense until I looked a second time. This time, I saw that it was, in fact, a chart pinpointing the exact location and racial breakdown of the voters in Perai.

I found myself fascinated by the numbers and soon forgot Rani Ibrahim's speech. Here was the constituency laid bare. I had gone to Butterworth by night and it had seemed haunting, ragged and only half-built. Suddenly, however, the roads I'd driven along assumed a greater meaning. I felt how I imagine a Chinese fortune-teller must feel when a client first presents himself – utterly ignorant, only to discover the web of history, fortune and the future embedded in the numbers given to him.

I saw that Jalan Assumption had the largest concentration of Malay voters – a delightful irony given the very Catholic-ness of the name; that Taman Chai Leng was the largest Chinese ward with nearly 20% of the seat's voting population; and that the wards of Prai and Kg Jawa Baru were the Indian redoubts – a very important factor in this seat where both candidates were Indian.

As I finished scanning the numbers, I felt I understood this mixed community – a community where the Chinese population was almost entirely balanced by an equal number of Malays and Indians, a balance which gave Barisan its glimmer of hope.

It was only then that I realised that the exact same process had been carried out for every constituency in the country; that the hands of a fortune-teller, so to speak, had been passed over every city, every small town, every kampung and every hamlet.

Driving through the constituency on the way to another *ceramah*, I was caught in a minor traffic jam caused, as it happened, by a DAP *ceramah*. As my car slowed to a crawl, I wound down the window only to catch the words of the DAP candidate, P. Patto, in full flow.

It was impassioned stuff and the audience was lapping it up. The Umno *ceramah* had been poorly attended by comparison: a hundred to a few hundred at the DAP one. As I drove on, I talked to Zahrain Hashim, a burly but mildly-spoken Penang Umno division head. He shook his head tiredly.

"Barisan *ceramahs* are always less well attended. You can hear our leaders on the TV or read about them in the newspapers. The DAP leaders don't have the same kind of exposure. The people have to attend if they want to know what they are thinking. I don't think it means they support them: it's a combination of curiosity and entertainment."

The mood at each *ceramah* may have been different but I suspect the *semangat* underlying may have been the same as both parties felt their way through the sea of numbers in search of that elusive prey – victory.

Follow The Leader

The Sun: Ceritalah
22 April 1995

For the past two weeks, I've been tying myself in knots as I try to be both fair and yet objective about Dr Mahathir: damning with faint praise or praising with faint damning, depending on how you look at it. This week, I'm writing about his deputy and anointed successor, Datuk Seri Anwar lbrahim. Having said that, I'd expect you, the reader, to remember that all writers have their preferences.

As a product of the establishment, you won't find me destroying the very society and world I belong to. I will point towards its failings and weaknesses. If you want more than that, you're going to have to turn to *The Rocket* or *Aliran Monthly* – two very fine, if opinionated, journals. They're the heavy artillery while I'm a sniper.

But back to the subject at hand: I'd like to talk about Anwar by drawing comparisons and contrasts between him and the PM. On the surface, as I think you'll agree, there's very little that links the two men except for the obvious: vast amounts of ambition and energy.

Anwar has used his personal charm as a rapier-like weapon, wielding it on the different communities in turn: businessmen, foreign investors, the Chinese, Indians, Kadazan or, with great difficulty, the Kelantanese. His handling of the Chinese community has been so deft, it's been quite staggering.

I find that listening to him quoting Confucius' maxims sends shivers down my spine, No, I don't feel betrayed. Quite the opposite. At last, I think, a Malay politician who is making an active effort to woo the Chinese community and not through money. He is reaching out to them by showing respect for their beliefs and their culture.

By way of comparison, Mahathir has always been more confrontational and aggressive. I like that. He's tough and combative.

Ask a stupid question and he'll put you in your place. The foreign media think of him as a wild card, at least in diplomatic terms. I differ in that I think he's a lot more straightforward than his successor. Anwar's charm (as we will learn over the years to come) masks a multitude of conflicting emotions and passions. In many ways, we will never know Anwar in the same way as we know Mahathir. In a country like Malaysia, where so much of our society depends on the leader for instruction and direction, there will be a definite change in atmosphere and tone.

Both men differ in terms of personality. And yet, despite that, they both share one very interesting characteristic, one which any future Umno leader should bear in mind if he or she has serious aspirations to lead this country. Both men are, or rather were, iconoclasts. Both of them were willing to stand outside the parameters of condoned behaviour and public opinion. And in each case, they championed issues which were to become highly important, if not all important, to the country.

In the case of Mahathir, it was the question of Malay rights and the need to redress decades of neglect, ignorance and poverty. His outspoken advocacy of Malay rights and his book *The Malay Dilemma* earned him the enmity of the then elite. However, the wisdom and timeliness of what he advocated was soon understood and, after a period in the wilderness, he was returned to the Umno fold.

Anwar has also demonstrated a similar willingness to take a stand. He has acquired a degree of credibility and stature because of his outspokenness during his university days. In his case, the issues were rural poverty and Islam – two issues that were to bedevil the country for much of the '70s. By bringing Anwar into Umno, Mahathir pre-empted a far greater problem, and one which was to destroy the Shah's Iran – the problem of balancing economic growth, modernisation, Islam and urbanisation.

While both men have been chastised for the radicalism they espoused in their early years, I feel the experience of being an outsider has served them extremely well, preparing them for their years in government. They stand apart from the bulk of the Umno elite in that they do generate ideas and policies.

Quite frankly, it's difficult to see who among the Umno elite (with a few notable exceptions) could be capable of such determination and direction. Besides generating policies, both men have been, in the main, able to implement and then execute the same policies.

Here though, I'll have to add some criticisms: the self-defeating rejection of the English language in the mid-'70s, the continuing confusion of our education system, the evil hand of political factionalism and excessive patronage, the continuing existence of the ISA, and the kindergarten we call the national media.

To be frank, we have little chance of altering what is a done deal. When the time comes, there will be the transition from PM to DPM and that will be that. We will clap our hands on the sidelines and then go back to work. Under normal circumstances, I would complain like hell because I don't feel that I, as a Malaysian voter, have had very much say in the appointment and selection of the next PM. However, the man chosen is bright, intelligent, well-read, ambitious and determined – all the ingredients needed for the job. My concern now lies with the question: who will the DPM be looking to in turn to succeed him?

PM's Perfect Pitch In DAP Moral Turf

The Sun
23 April 1995

There are times when I wonder whether there was a political life before Dr Mahathir? As an English-educated Malaysian, I'm so used to being criticised by him, I half-cringe in anticipation whenever I see him on TV. I feel as if I've spent most of my life at the receiving end of his withering sarcasm.

He overwhelms the political landscape by dint of his longevity and energy. However, after years of listening to him hectoring me, telling me what to do and generally bossing me around, I've noticed, at least during this election, a slightly more amenable tone. And here, in Penang – a state which is proving to be the real test of the past five years in office – Dr Mahathir is actively seeking, even pleading for the support of the voters.

Maybe I'm reading too much into his recent visit, but in Tanjung Tokong on Friday night, amid a crowd of thousands (a crowd that equalled the DAP's *ceramah*, both in size and spirit), I discovered Mr Nice Guy. Of course, if you were Mat Sabu or Lim Kit Siang, you might disagree and, to be quite frank, I was pretty surprised, too.

So why's he trying to be Mr Nice Guy? The answer's simple.

Penang's truculence has disturbed the Barisan juggernaut. The DAP's momentum in the state has surprised people, especially given the buoyancy of the state economy. In Barisan parlance, the DAP has no issues and it's true, it doesn't appear to have substantive economic issues.

What it does have, however, is the high moral ground of democratic rights and freedom, as well as the extremely unpopular head of the Penang Island Municipal Council, Tan Gim Hwa – issues it has been exploiting for all their worth. But then, this is an election and issues are there, wailing to be tackled.

The neat simplicity of the racial arguments in Penang tends to obscure the complex factors that have made these issues so current. Because as voters (of all races) become more prosperous, they want more in the way of democratic rights and freedom. For example, on the evening I attended the DAP *ceramah*, a Taiwanese activist spoke at great length about the struggle to have an opposition politician elected to the mayoral office of Taipeh. His speech was warmly received because his cry for greater truth and justice struck a resonant chord in the audience.

Penang, then, presents a glitch in the Malaysian Dream as propounded by Mahathir – proof, ironically, of his own success. Development, according to the Barisan formula, is supposed to appease the population and turn them into loyal supporters. The people who work in the Free Trade Zones are supposed to go to work and then spend their money at Bayan Baru's shopping complex, Sunshine Square, sipping root beer whilst chomping on croissants. It does work, at least for a while. However, after a certain point, the populace begins to treat the government like a service that may or may not need to be privatised. They've seen how the performance of Telekom and Tenaga have improved through competition. This makes them think. Surely governments could do with the same measure of competition? Almost inevitably, a more affluent population has higher expectations of government.

So, was there a change in the PM's tone? Well, I think there was. For a start, the Prime Minister's speeches were studded with references to the rule of law, to the issue of accountability and – when referring to Dr Koh Tsu Koon – the importance of having a humane, thoughtful and yet performance-orientated chief minister. He wasn't telling us what to think so much as selling the services of his management team. In business terms, he was making a 'pitch', a pitch which is targeted at the DAP's high moral ground, which, in many ways, was a fairly cheeky undertaking from the man who ordered Operation Lallang.

However, this pitch cannot be made in his usual combative, take-it-or-leave-it style. In Penang, the PM has toned down his presentation. At Tanjung Bunga – Koh's embattled state seat – the PM was conciliatory, all-embracing and, at times, even funny. I remember scratching my head and asking myself: Is this my PM?

As the Barisan flags were waved, as children played in the trees, as the Punjabi *bhangra* group rehearsed their steps, the PM changed in front of my eyes. For the first time, for me at least, he came across as a man with a sense of humour and warmth, turning his opponent, Kit Siang, into the automaton – Robocop. Penang has forced this change on the PM. He wants to win here, full stop. And, like any politician who wants to win, he has to gauge what his audience wants to hear, combining their interests with the standard BN fare. The rule of law, democracy and human rights have never been the PM's favourite rallying points. Maybe this is changing? I hope so, but then maybe I'm too hopeful.

Uneasiness Over Thought Of Change

The Sun

24 April 1995

When I first hatched the idea of hitting the road and covering the country during the ten days of the election campaign, it seemed nothing more to me than a pleasant tour – a gentle stroll through towns, both familiar and unknown. I hadn't planned to face up to any great challenges because political upheavals along the way seemed highly unlikely. As far as I could see, the results themselves were a foregone conclusion.

I was going to write 'mood' pieces – slices of life, quirky, personal and hopefully, insightful. Well, I was wrong. After staying in Penang for four days on the road, my precious peace of mind was shattered. The previous two stops in Kuching and Johor Bahru had reaffirmed what I thought to be the country's essential contentment with the BN government. These visits did nothing to stir the blood, though the potential I saw in young leaders like Hishammuddin Hussein Onn and Halimah Mohamed Sadique gave me hope for my generation.

Penang, however, was a shock – the flags, the Fortuna Restaurant packed to the gills, the *ceramahs* and the passion. Instead of writing neat little vignettes, I found myself utterly confused and depressed because my journey, the real journey – the journey that has taught me about myself and my country – only really began in the island state. On the eve of my departure from Penang, I now admit that Penang has shaken me up and disturbed my preconceptions. It has shown me the flaws of my world view and the limitations of being a bleeding heart liberal. Why Penang? Because in Penang, I discovered the voters had a choice and a choice they were seriously contemplating.

As a journalist, I should have been thrilled to be living in such exciting times, reporting on the day-to-day nuances of a campaign that might change the face of Malaysian politics. But I was not. I was not excited because I discovered that I was afraid of that choice – afraid of the leap into the unknown. My fear was not because I suspected Lim Kit Siang of being a racist. Neither was I disturbed by the DAP's Malay candidates. I was afraid of the possibility of change. It was as simple as that.

I had gotten so used to the idea of continuity, stability and prosperity that change was an anathema. Change itself was a threat. Change meant the unknown and I was afraid of the unknown. My reasons for being afraid were not laudable and I was unimpressed by myself for holding them. I should have been brave. I should have been strong. As a writer, I knew I was privileged to be living in exciting times. However, as a Malaysian, I don't want to be living in exciting times. I'd be lying if I said anything else.

Despite my misgivings about the possibility of change, I do understand one thing. We Malaysians must get used to that same possibility. Conflicting views are not in themselves dangerous. It is the inability to accept the contrary, the unwillingness to accept dialogue that leads to chaos. We have to learn to see change as something potentially positive. We have changed our nation and ourselves, socially and culturally. We must get used to the idea of change in a political context. The freedom of choice we wish to exercise in economic terms cannot be uncoupled from the democratic freedoms. We can hold it off and try to introduce it gradually. That's fine, but at the end of the day, it will come and we must be prepared for it.

Having said that, the brevity of the campaign period telescopes nearly five years of national and state grouses into ten frantic days. It makes for an intoxicating brew and exaggerates emotions and issues. Nonetheless, I feel Penang has become the lightning conductor for the nation, a test of the Mahathir years. Political life in Malaysia is harsh and the winners do take all. Let us hope that through their struggle, whatever the outcome, the nation emerges more mature.

Not Stupid And They Want Respect

The Sun
25 April 1995

Well over 30,000 people were crammed into Kota Bharu's Stadium Sultan Mohamed IV to hear Tok Guru Datuk Nik Aziz and Tengku Razaleigh Hamzah – leaders of PAS and Parti Melayu Semangat 46 respectively – speak. Men, women and children bobbed up and down as the speakers made their points. Looking around me I saw that the stands were full and that latecomers were crowded into a corner of the stadium by the main entrance. As I was looking around, the entire stadium suddenly rose to its feet to read out a short declaration.

The voice of the man leading the declaration (which had been distributed to the crowd) was shrill. There were a litany of straightforward points – that Islam and the Syariah were the basis of Kelantan's administration, that the Kelantanese were not stupid, that they would not sell their state, or pawn their future.

As the man concluded, he cried out *Allahuakhbar*! three times, punching the sky in his exuberance. Had there been a roof to the stadium, it would have been lifted off by those cries. Observing the excitement, I was reminded of a moment a few nights earlier in Penang when Lim Kit Siang's arrival at the Fortuna Hotel had been accompanied by a sudden blast of music. Shivering at the memory and the disconcerting parallels, I turned my attention to the speaker, Nik Aziz.

Nik Aziz, Kelantan's Mentri Besar, has been the object of enormous media criticism. Ever sceptical of press coverage, I was curious to find out for myself what the man was like. Listening to him speak, I was surprised by his balance and reasonableness, though I must add that as long as he spoke in Malay I understood him. Whenever he slipped into Kelantanese, I lost the thread of his argument. Nonetheless, I couldn't help marvelling at the vibrancy and vigour of the Kelantanese. Despite the inroads of Bahasa Baku, TV3 and the national press, the Kelantanese had still managed to cling on to their cultural roots – their essential 'differentness' – and I respected them for that. Nik Aziz (just as Razaleigh was to, later in the evening) criticised the press coverage of his home state and the many run-ins he'd had with the federal authorities. However, he stressed his success at working with people of other races and religions.

And though he was only the size of a postage stamp at the far side of a large stadium, I, for one, felt sympathy for the man. Sympathy and respect, however, is not agreement because the experiment being conducted in Kelantan is based, to a large extent, on state parochialism and prejudice. And these are emotions and passions that I have always found untenable in the national scope of things. Maybe I'm too much of a 'One Malaysian' to see their value. I can see their cultural and linguistic importance but I am skeptical about the political relevance. Whatever it was, the arguments raging in my head once again reminded me of those I'd encountered in Sabah and even in Penang.

The Kelantanese, much like the Sabahans in the mid-'80s, had had enough of the federal government's attitude both towards them and their leaders. Having been with Joseph Pairin Kitingan in the Kadazan-Dusun heartland of Keningau on nomination day, I saw numerous parallels between the two states – both at the margins of the nation's political and economic life.

Both states had moved into the opposition because of a dislike for federal leaders or their proxies. Having made that move, they were vilified for their decision. No attempt was made to win them back. No attempt was made to find out why they disdained the centre. Punishment was the only response: harsh, unwarranted and self-defeating. My dream of a 'One Malaysia' chucked into the *longkang* like a bit of rubbish. The torrent of criticism and the slanted media coverage only made people more antagonistic towards KL and the whole idea of Malaysia.

During lunch earlier that day with some old family friends, I noted the resentment in my hosts' voices as they spoke of the media's presentation of their home state.

"Karim, I want you to realise: We're neither stupid nor backward. Look at us. We are a proud people and such claims only turn us against the Barisan. I dare you to write that. You Barisan types from KL are going to have to learn to respect us."

Stunned by their bitterness, I held my tongue. The more I thought on the matter, the more I sensed a deep-rooted complacency at work: a disregard for the limbs of the nation. In many ways, I had been just as culpable as the political class. Locked away in KL, I had sought to impose my KL-centric views on politics and economics, whether it was in Sabah, Penang or Kelantan. I had not stopped to think what the people in each of these states might have wanted. Nor had I tried to think of ways of accommodating them within the ambit of the nation.

Electorate Confound The Pundits

The Sun
27 April 1995

On a day when the heavens opened and flooded many of the roads in the Klang valley, the country went to the polls. After ten days of frenetic campaigning, the politicians sat back nervously to await the *rakyat's* final say. I had thought it would be very close: a cliffhanger of sorts with the DAP, PAS, Semangat 46 and PBS snapping at Barisan's heels.

I was wrong, very wrong – proof that so-called political columnists such as myself can completely misread the mood of the country. Having followed the campaign trail from Sabah through Sarawak, Johor, Penang and Kelantan, I had missed the reality on the ground which was – 'business as usual'.

Waiting in the lobby of Menara Tun Hussein at the PWTC from 9.30 pm, I had a long time to reflect on my misreading of the campaign. I studied the marble floors, the echoing concrete fastnesses and looked quizzically at the lifts that took the really important people up to the 39th floor where the PM was awaiting the result.

It was then that I started trying to figure out where I'd gone wrong. Had I been too close to the electioneering? Had I lost my objectivity? Was I just stupid? Whatever it was, I suspected that I was not alone because many of the other journalists looked on with amazement at the results that poured in.

And no result was more keenly anticipated than Dr Koh Tsu Koon's. His victory, so early in the evening, had started off my bout of self-criticism and self-evaluation, robbing the evening of its climax. I had expected a long drawn out affair – like the previous election's Thriller in Padang Kota. Perhaps I should have known better. After all, I had been to his constituency and observed him. He was obviously a decent, hard-working man. I had seen the posh new UDA flats in his state constituency, the roads and the cheering crowds and whilst I'd wanted him to win, I hadn't been confident of his ability to swing enough votes to the coalition.

Of course, Barisan's victory was never in doubt and most of the journalists hanging around downstairs were more concerned with the details: the margin of the victories, the majorities, Mat Sabu and Kelantan. The two-thirds majority was, likewise, never in doubt. Thinking about the details, I remembered what one minister had said to me some 35,000 ft in the air.

He had said: "It's the margin of victory that matters, not the victory itself. We must have a ringing endorsement. There are many difficult challenges ahead of us and we must have a strong government." Well, he was right and I conceded the point to him in retrospect. At the time, I thought it was straightforward election talk.

So what can I say about the victory as I saw it at 3 am, whilst sipping bitter tea from a polystyrene cup in the lobby of the Menara Tun Hussein Onn ?

First of all, I have to mention the sheer overwhelming scale of the victory. This election must surely have witnessed one of the most staggering swings to Barisan, the incumbent government, ever. There were seats as unprepossessing as Telok Intan in Perak (held by MCA's Ong Ka Ting) which leapt from being a simple 2,000 or so majority to a 14,000 majority, a trend that was repeated by MIC deputy president Datuk S.S. Subramaniam in Segamat.

What does this swing mean? It means that you, the electorate, have given the Barisan a resounding victory. It's not a qualified endorsement. It's clear, unqualified and unequivocal. It's as if the PM is being told – "you've done a good job. Now, get on and do the rest." I can't say anything else. I still have my criticisms about the Barisan government. However, it seems churlish for me to talk about them now when the electorate has given the PM such a clear sign of support.

Perhaps the most exciting aspect of the results is the very clear sign of a swing to the government from the Chinese voting population. In seats with large Chinese vote-banks, the swing to BN appears to be extraordinarily strong. In Bukit Mertajam, a DAP majority of over a thousand was turned into a 11,000 Barisan majority.

These figures were repeated across the nation, showing the Chinese community's support for BN. In fact, I suspect it's been their support that's made the vast leap possible because Kelantan was a patchy night for the coalition. The 1995 election will go down in history as a watershed for Barisan. Could it be the moment when Barisan finally won the unequivocal support of the Chinese community?

The Purview Of Politics

The Sun: Ceritalah

29 April 1995

The Malaysian elections are not about fairplay or justice – they're about winning. In this game, winner does take all. You cannot run away from the brutal reality of the system as the DAP's Dr Kua Kia Soong found to his dismay on nomination day. It's unpalatable and ugly, especially for those of us brought up on the verities of one man one vote and democratic ideals.

There was a time, to my eyes, when the entire system seemed riddled by corruption, hypocrisy and manipulation. I wouldn't say that these have disappeared, because they haven't. In certain cases, they've gotten worse. Nonetheless, the anger and disgust I used to feel, especially in the late '80s, when I was a young lawyer, has abated. I now see things differently.

The Malaysian political structure is based on the presumption that man cannot be trusted. The argument runs as follows: men and women, will, especially if they're divided by race, religion, language or culture, do their utmost to exacerbate these differences. Violence, as a result, is never far from the surface.

This view is contrary to the Western ideal, which sees man as being inherently noble and good, except when he is subjected to the evil force of interfering governments and meddlesome politicians. As a result, I am appalled by the sharp disparity between the political process as it exists in Malaysia – the woeful level of public debate in the Dewan Rakyat – and the ideals that I was taught to hold in such high esteem. What I've now discovered is that these ideals may not be relevant, at least at the moment, to Malaysia. It's taken me a long time to reach this conclusion and it's been a long, exhausting journey, both physically and politically – a journey that began on nomination day.

Standing in the midst of a fiercely-proud crowd of Kadazans in Keningau, I remember wondering what it was that kept these simple padi farmers so loyal to Pairin Kitingan when his henchmen – Bernard Dompok, Joseph Kurup – jumped parties at the drop of a hat.

Had Pairin's policy of confrontation with the federal government benefited the Kadazans? I don't think so. His people were fast becoming a minority in their own state, their constituencies subtly redelineated. He had chosen the high road without factoring in the brute force and power of Kuala Lumpur. Pairin had failed to see that his people's best interests were better served through consultation and accommodation. Politics in Malaysia is about the art of the possible. It shouldn't be about leading your people into a wilderness.

Having been on the road since nomination day, I've come to see Malaysia as a country of nearly 20 million very different people – a polity in name but not in much else. Frankly, the diversity within our boundaries makes no sense. If we allowed everybody free rein, the centrifugal forces might destroy the precious security and stability we now enjoy. The problem hitherto has been my KL-centric, middle-class world view. I lived in a world that was hermetic and self-contained. Basically, I've been thinking "surely everyone else thinks the same as me?" Well, they don't.

Hitting the campaign trail has taught me how foolish I have been. Why then do we still get excited about the whole process? Why was Georgetown festooned with banners and posters like a Hindu bride on her wedding day? Quite simply, it's because the people themselves still relish the fight, the display of political aggression, not to mention the chance that their vote (at least in Penang) may influence their future lives. The elections do provide a special forum, perhaps the only forum, to air grievances. It's a vital opportunity to let off steam.

Having trailed across Malaysia from one end to another – from *ceramahs* held at the foot of Mount Kinabalu, on the banks of the

Kuching river, in the depths of Johor's oil palm estates, to Georgetown and Kota Bharu – I've come away with the realisation that the electoral process is alive. I have no doubt about that. Though heavily weighted in favour of the Barisan, the elections are a test of the Government's mandate.

It's not a question of whether or not they are going to win. We all know the answer to that question. Nonetheless, the Government is in search of a mandate, of the sanction of the people, their agreement and concordance. The two-thirds majority is a hurdle that the PM knows he must clear effortlessly. Anything less and he knows that he's faced with a truculent population that is ready and willing to take him on, face to face.

What we have to do, however, is start to see the whole process – and not just the elections – outside the prism of what a Western liberal democracy would call a democracy. Our elections are our own. This may sound nonsensical. Surely all elections are *sui generis* – true to themselves, the people, their culture and their community.

We in Malaysia are creating a different political language, and a whole new set of political reference points. We are inventing the wheel in terms of race relations and religious integration, as well as the democratic structure that holds the whole apparatus together. I might sound like a Government apologist but there's no doubt in my mind that the harsh realities of race, religion and culture require equally harsh politics. The political structure that we have has evolved out of the specific conditions of our world. It is not imposed from above. It has grown – through trial and error. Being the Prime Minister of Malaysia does not mean you are a law unto yourself. You are circumscribed by factors that limit your ambit of action. The elections of 1995 are merely a crude reflection of these truths.

Roots

Roots

New Straits Times Annual 1994

When my father was killed in a car crash, I was a little boy answering the telephone. I was seven years old. It was a Sunday. My father and mother had taken the Lamborghini and gone out for a drive – my father would have said to *makan angin*, literally to eat air, words that now haunt me with a stubborn malevolence. The house was left in our charge, my two brothers and I. The servants were either asleep or out, enjoying the day off.

The house was not left undisturbed for long. Within half an hour, the telephone started ringing incessantly, hot with anxious callers – 'Had we heard?', 'Where were they taking the body?', 'How was my mother?' I can remember answering the telephone calls until dusk when an uncle arrived, much shaken by the news, to take charge of us.

Evening saw the house alive with faces, a few familiar, that smiled warmly and reassuringly whenever we walked by. Solemn, sad faces that flashed into view like a cinefilm. I say like cinefilm because my father was a great enthusiast, shooting the family with unflagging spirits. And for want of real memories, I have often had to watch the films again and again, reliving my childhood through celluloid until the fading shots of my fifth birthday party have been embedded in my own memories and become muddled with what, if anything, was originally there.

There are times when what I remember seems as jerky and awkward as a hand-held cine-camera with all the random swings to the left and right that characterised my father's passion for celluloid. But it has meant that I can replay a memory, rewinding it, fast-forwarding it, enjoying the players' discomfort as they leap out of swimming pools and relight birthday cakes with a puff of air.

And that night's memories are no different – Uncle Noni, walking into the viewfinder and then out again, the cine-camera moving hastily, accommodating him into the field of vision as he filled the brass braziers that were to surround the body with smoking incense. I can remember peeking through the banisters, watching the mourners arrive, the women with their heads covered.

A hush fell over the crowd when my father's remains, shrouded in white, were brought into the house. And it is here that what memories I do have have failed me entirely (perhaps the motor of the cine-camera finally expired, the battery dead – I don't know) and I have had to resort, in part, to what others have told me subsequently. It infuriates me now not to know the smallest details of the day's events.

As for crash itself – the cause of death – for many years, it remained unexplained and undescribed, a moment my mother never referred to. When, in heavy traffic, her hands gripped the steering wheel with an unaccustomed firmness and she started biting her lower lip, all of us understood the memory that haunted her, though not its contents.

Perhaps it was thought that the truth would be too ugly, too disturbing – something that would haunt our nights – when, in fact, it was not the truth that is disturbing but the absence of the truth and the machinations of the imagination as it tries to flesh out the whole story, unassisted.

Finally, last year, I found out what happened. My father had overtaken a sluggish lorry only to find himself in the path of another lorry. He had tried to brake. The car had gone into a somersault, something the makers had promised it would never do. My mother, by some miracle, had been able to clamber out of the Lamborghini seconds after it had completed its gymnastics. She fought to open his door but it had jammed.

A crowd gathered to gawp at the sight. No one helped her. The car ran on high-octane gas fuel. It exploded minutes later and she was blown back in the blast. Friends have assured me that my father was killed on impact. But I cannot banish from my mind the possibility that he was alive, concussed perhaps, but alive.

'The family' – uncles and aunts, cousins, nephews and grandun-cles – must have been at a loss as to how to deal with the three of us. As a result, we spent much of the early evening being shuttled from house to house until it was decided, by committee, to drive us back to my father's home town for the burial the next day.

That night, the cars assembled at the house for the drive to Kuala Kangsar, just as they had always done, except that my father was not there to give orders, nor my mother there to fuss. I remember the smell of the red leather seats in the Jaguar and the feel of the thin cotton blankets. We were bundled into the back of the car and Kam, my younger brother, cried for much of the journey because his *amah* had to be left behind.

We left Kuala Lumpur and headed north on the Ipoh road past a roundabout lit by amber lights. I see it now as my first journey – a journey in time and culture, through a landscape separating me from my past and the traditions that had encompassed the family through the generations. It was my first journey, a journey that took me back to my father's home, my grandfather's world and my past – returning along the road that each had taken in turn, escaping in their own way the narrow confines of their hometown, Kuala Kangsar. Though, in my case, the drive back that night was to mark a 'break', a transition of sorts that would make all subsequent less familiar and less known.

The rest of the journey is shrouded in mist though I have traced and retraced the highway a hundred times subsequently – past or-dered plantations of rubber trees and stumpy oil palms, jerry-built shophouses laid out on a grid, each little more than a ribbon of brick and mortar beaten out of a lowland forest. The contours of the land, the towns and the rivers have assumed familiarity but the men who once plied the roads – my father and grandfather – remained distant and 'unknowable'. That night, the towns were flashes of light seen from the back of the car, dull and indistinct in the inky-blue night.

Ipoh must have been stirring by the time we drove through its wide streets; the early risers performing their ritual ablutions before the first prayers of the day, others making coffee, and the Chinese stallholders at work, chopping up boiled chicken – pink and bloody to the touch of the chopstick. We drove on, oblivious: Kuala Kangsar was only 30 miles away. We might have driven along Gopeng Road past the State Secretary's residence, the family home for many years.

Kuala Kangsar was my father's home town, his kampung, my kampung and his resting place, though to say it is to risk admitting my ignorance of the skein of life that had brought me to this town. Kuala Kangsar was where he grew up, a 'Royal' town, home to the Sultans of Perak and their Court. My father was the eldest son of a man who struck fear and apprehension into all he encountered, not least the Sultan. And yet, my father never lived with his father. Instead, he was cared for by his uncle. It was a Malay custom of the time (or perhaps a custom peculiar to Perak) that the eldest son should be entrusted to the care of his most senior uncle. It must have broken my grandmother's heart – a woman who died long before my birth. She was a dutiful woman and would never have thought to dispute the claim. For many years thereafter, when my grandmother visited her son with presents or clothes she had made for him, he would call her the 'tailor', knowing no better.

The town lies 30 miles or so to the northwest of Ipoh, across a plain blighted by open-cast tin mines – a wounded expanse of slag heaps and murky mining pools. A bridge spans the Perak river and the village of Kota Lama emerges from behind the emerald canopy. Kota Lama soon merges into the town, or what there is of it, and its two notable features: the clock tower that never works and the large mansion, once occupied by the British Resident, that commands the bluff overlooking the town and the sinuous river. A river that was once forded many years ago by one of our servants on the eve of his nuptials after he had set eyes on the woman he was to marry. The town appears to have changed only very slightly since the days when an English novelist and schoolteacher, Anthony Burgess, strode about its streets in search of warm Anchor beer.

This is not my Kuala Kangsar, my 'KK'. When I think of KK, I remember the cemetery of the Ubadiah mosque which is full of family graves, intermingled with those of the Perak royal families. I remember funerals and family gatherings, and men and women who had never ventured outside KK. I think back to a time of certainty and order, generations of men who ruled by right, and ruled well, if harshly. History, blood and death, men and women whose past lives I have reconstructed in an attempt to glean an understanding of myself.

Perak history has been forged in steel; in different steels: the rifles and the cannons of the British and the swirling krises of the Malays. The kris is a short, flat sword with a true blade and a jagged edge. They protect their masters from evil and divine the future. All have slight blemishes of texture and colour. The Perakian kris would betray the traces of the many adventurers that weighed anchor off her coast – Indian merchants from Kalinga, Arabs, Sumatrans, and Bugis privateers.

The Bugis first arrived in the 1840s. At their head were the men of my family. They came from the Celebes, by way of Batavia, Borneo, Riau and Malacca, settling in Perak at the behest of the Sultan, fighting men, kris-bearing, who now longed for a more settled way of life, to wed and have children. The translucent mark of the Bugis suffuses the kris, lending a richness and auroral tinge appropriate for men who themselves came from the east.

Professional fighters are rarely controllable and these settlers became a byword for 'brigandry and dacoity' as the British would have said. They were involved in the murder of the priggish British Resident, James Wheeler Woodford Birch, while he was bathing, on November 2, 1875. The culprits were hanged and the sympathisers banished.

The violent and bloody suppression by the British that same year left all the villages along the Perak river smouldering and the ranks of the Perak nobles decimated. The protagonists were hung;

the conspirators exiled to the Seychelles and the Cape (where many of their descendants still remain). It was after this blood-letting and amidst the intrigues of the Istana that the first of my family received his hereditary Dato'ship.

His name was Jaragan Abdul Shukor, and he was my grandfather's grandfather. Almost unbelievably, his youngest child is still alive. She lives in an old wooden house in Ipoh; her face still wreathed in the most exquisite and serene of smiles. I am her great-grandnephew. She was married into the wealthy Panglima Kinta family that received revenues from all the tin mined in the vicinity of Ipoh. Her husband is long dead and still her face is imbued with a saintliness and calm that her 80 years have not dampened.

Her father, Jaragan, was a man of fixed intention and determination. His powers, temporal, spiritual and magical, were great. A mosque on the river was built by him alone – the great beams that straddled its roof summoned from out of the river by the majesty of his voice.

Stories have been passed down of how he placed charms on the tree trunks and stone slabs that miraculously arranged themselves into a mosque. The mosque still stands. My uncles and aunts have all been there to pray. None, I believe, has since experienced the serenity and peace of mind they felt in that place. The family still possesses krises from that time: krises that are magical, that select their own masters. One uncle foolishly tried to keep the krises after they had already chosen his brother as their master. He was struck down with a malarial fever. When the krises were delivered into the hands of their rightful owner, he was made well again. But this happened long after my father's death and I must not run ahead of my journey.

The funeral was hot and stuffy – once again sensations, sensations: hot and cold, dampness and dryness, but no emotion. We had been woken and dressed by our aunts – marshalled into our ill-fitting *baju Melayu*. I remember being sat on a chair, in the shade. I cried uncontrollably. That I remember – thank God! But did I cry because I knew my father was dead? Did I? I don't think so. I think I was beyond tears, beyond understanding. My younger brother, who was only three at the time, also cried, more out of fear and tiredness. He must have been missing his *amah* Lily. One aunt whose husband was stationed deep in the jungle arrived at the funeral with fistfuls of her hair in her hands.

My mother was not there because she was still in the hospital recovering from the accident. It is not impossible that I thought that she, too, had died and that her body was also being lowered into the same grave. I was told by a family friend only last year that my father had been buried in an outsized coffin. I had not understood what he meant. He explained to me reluctantly that because my father's body had been burnt in the blaze, the body had hardened into the position he had been in when driving. It was, he said, a Malay custom not to break the bones of the corpse to facilitate the burial. One great-aunt had been so shocked by the size of the coffin that she had fainted.

We returned to grandfather's house after the burial. We used to call him Dato', the Malay word for grandfather, which was also his hereditary title. Dato' had died only the year before and his stern, forbidding presence still clung to the rooms. Perhaps because my memories of the house are, in the main, happy ones, I cannot think of it without being inundated with curry puffs, *bifstik*, servants sleeping on the kitchen floor, solar topees and stuffed hornbills.

It was a large 'modern-style bungalow' that had been marvelled at when first built. Some thought it was too close to the main road and perhaps not airy enough. They were right. The lorries that rattled along the main road shook the house and the louvre windows and the intricate brickwork that was intended to ventilate the communal rooms failed in their task.

We, the grandchildren, had loved staying there when he was alive. The cupboards and shelves bore the trophies of the past: enormous stuffed hornbills that fell on top of you if you opened the wardrobe in the master bedroom; discarded school books still fresh with the teacher's remarks – 'Noordin, where is your homework?'; bolts of gaudy silk; faded *Korans* reverentially stored; Dato's solar topee; a treasured kris; Malay film magazines with pictures of a pouting Siput Sarawak; MCKK (Malay College Kuala Kangsar) school ties and sports cups.

Quite apart from the hidden delights of the house, many of which were strictly forbidden us, there was always Kak Masa and Pak Abid, the couple who lived in the shabby wooden house behind the kitchens. They had innumerable children and the house shook whenever they were all in it at once. Kak Masa cooked and cleaned for my grandmother; Pak Abid delegated and since he had eight children, the delegation remained remarkably straightforward.

My father used to call him 'Andy Capp' after the cartoon character. Kak Masa looked Chinese. She had a mole on her chin. There was a long hair that grew out of it which she refused to pluck. Her hair was tied up in a bun that loosened as the day went on. When we were all there, it fell out inevitably by midday.

Kak Masa held sway in the kitchen. Request for food had to be made to her. She would try to be firm, but being soft-hearted by nature, she could never refuse giving each of us a sliver of whatever she might be making. Her *kuih* or cakes were legendary and the afternoons were the best time to descend on the kitchen. There were the brightly coloured jellies, turquoise and green; agar-agar, cakes made from rice flour flavoured with coconut milk and molasses that exploded in your mouth, as did the curry puffs which were served with scaldingly hot chilli sauce.

The house now stands empty. It is difficult to find tenants and clothes mildew in the wardrobes. Pak Abid and Kak Masa have long moved to their own concrete house, bought with the money my mother gave them before she took us back to England. My family have long since moved to Kuala Lumpur and visit Kuala Kangsar infrequently.

The change has been sudden.

Perak was my grandfather's world, its boundaries, his boundaries; its people, his people. He was a man of custom and tradition, who respected the *adat* as much as the sanctions of the *Koran*. Position was by right of birth; democracy and meritocracy, words and concepts entirely alien to his vocabulary and knowledge. When Tunku Abdul Rahman came to his house to offer Dato' a post in the Federal administration, Dato' had said yes. But his sojourn in Kuala Lumpur was short and he soon returned to Perak.

At the time no one was sure why he chose to relinquish his prestigious post in the capital for relative obscurity in Perak. Part of the reason, I like to think, was his reluctance to leave his state. He knew the land intimately. He had been stationed everywhere – in Dindings on the coast, Ipoh, Grik, deep in the interior. He understood his place in its history, but wanted no part in its future, perhaps because he understood that his time had passed. He felt only scorn for those who had risen to positions of power through the new political parties – men whose fathers had been simple farmers, artisans or schoolteachers. He was too proud to take orders from such people. His upbringing did not allow for such an usurpation of order.

My father grew up in the care of his childless uncle. Adopted at birth, he was later laid to rest in the shade of a magnolia tree beside his uncle's grave rather than with his father. His uncle was very particular about his education – he was allowed unlimited credit at all the booksellers in Kuala Kangsar and Ipoh. I still have a few of his books, those that escaped the white ants and the silverfish, each of them inscribed in his spidery hand. After so much attention, retainers that sat outside the classroom to fetch water for him and a chauffeur-driven Daimler to ferry him the half mile to and from school, it was not surprising that he won a scholarship to complete his studies in England.

He wanted to read law but had not been allowed to. Instead he became an accountant. I have a small picture of him, taken on the long voyage to Southampton. He looks tall; tall for a Malay (it must have been his Bugis blood), with his fashionable Oxford bags billowing at the knee. His London days are shrouded in mystery. He must have enjoyed them immensely – I keep on meeting men who knew him from those days, who chortle knowingly when they find out who I am, as if reliving memories of smoky pubs, student dances and dinners at Veeraswamys'. When he came back to Malaysia years later with an English wife and his professional qualification, he took a job in the capital. The provincial ways of KK and the gossip that floated through the town, much of it concerning his father and his family, made KK and Perak an intolerable place to live, especially for the modern man that he so obviously aspired to be.

He had never been close to his father. When Dato' took another wife (who, it had to be said, was as old or as young, depending on how you looked at it, as my mother), the relations between the two men, never close in the first place, became distant and strained. My father never forgave Dato' for what he did to his mother. He was sure, as were many others, that Dato' – the foolish old man – had been entrapped: she was in her twenties; he, in his sixties. My grandmother, in her misery, took to locking herself in her bedroom each night that Dato' was away.

Many years later, I was to meet the woman, discovering that a man could love two wives and that life was never as simple as one had hoped when young. But for my grandmother, the second marriage was tragic. For hours on end, she would cry – long deep wails that stilled the night and led to her death. On the rare nights Dato' spent at home, she would brighten. She would prepare his favourite dishes and dress to please him, but after nine confinements, Dato's indifference sapped her will to live. She died at the age of 46 and with her passing, the family lost what little semblance of harmony and happiness it had once possessed.

The old ways, the meetings with the *bomoh* or witchdoctor, the haughtiness of the nobles and their petty tyrannies was not what my father wanted to return to. His world, his dreams, were of development and progress: 'Good Government and Opportunity for All'. He was invited to join a discussion group called Forum. They knew they were men with foresight and vision. Forum wanted 'self-determination', 'national integrity' and an end to 'neo-colonialism'.

When they succeeded in ridding the country of the British, Malaysians would inherit their jobs and responsibilities. They had to raise the Malays from out of the kampungs and into the cities where they could compete with the Chinese and Indians; taking charge of their own destinies. A world seemed to await of Malay industrialists, doctors – yes, that doctor – administrators and leaders. The membership of the Forum reads like a 'Who's Who' of contemporary Malay life: judges, university professors, financiers and cabinet ministers. But they were not just interested in discussing serious matters. One weekend they took a bungalow at Port Dickson and shipped in dancing girls.

Finance was my father's chosen world and, in quick succession, he rose to become the first Malay accountant-general in the days when the Sultan Abdul Samad building had been the secretariat, sauntering across the Padang to the 'Spotted Dog' for his lunch. Later, he went on to found one of the country's largest banks at a time when the only Malays working in banks were the drivers and the *jagas*, as well as a now flourishing accountancy practice that still bears his name. He was 39 when he died.

Despite his success, he had always regretted never having gone to university. As if to compensate, he read voraciously – biography, contemporary politics and economics – books that I, as a young man, was to pore over in a desperate search for clues of his character and disposition, so vague and shady were my own memories. I know that it is because of him that I went on to university.

With the funeral over, we returned to Kuala Lumpur. The house in Kenny Hills still attracted visitors every day; soft-faced and tearful, they offered condolences to my mother and patted us on our heads. I can remember running past scores of bouquets – orchids, chrysanthemums and roses – that turned the house, for a few days only, into a melancholy florist. In the early evenings, men from the local mosque came to offer prayers for my father. The overpowering scent of the funeral bouquets, the murmured prayers of the men hunched over their open *Korans* and my mother's scarred face is all I can remember of those long days in the Kenny Hills house.

Within a year of my father's death, we left for England, my mother's home. The family had always approved of the public school system and we were each of us subjected to their vigours. I went on to Cambridge, as much for my father as for myself. At St Johns', I met one of my father's friends who was making a belated return to formal education. For weeks on end, the two of us talked until late into the night as I tried to retrace in my mind at least the outline of my father's face, fitting into it all the stories and anecdotes that I listened to. But the man still eluded me and all that I was left with was a cipher, as thin and transient as the mist that continued to obscure my view. It was not that I hadn't tried to find out about him. I had and, at times, almost obsessively so, listening to countless old friends, acquaintances and family members as they recounted their stories. However, the man remained distant and shadowy.

As I came to the end of my studies, the emptiness and hollowness of my memories taunted me time and again. I felt a deep-seated anger at him for leaving me in this irreconcilable ignorance. 'Why?' I would ask myself. 'Why did you leave me without explaining who you were and who I am, or rather, who I am supposed to be?'

The confusion I felt left me with no choice but to return home, knowing that as I did, there was no other place save Kuala Kangsar, where my tired bones in years to come, could be buried. Perhaps it was only by living out my fate amongst the half-remembered memories of my past, by living a life just as he did, that I would learn about him and then myself. Perhaps only then the mists would clear and the odd distancing sensations fall away, leaving the passion of grief and the relief of understanding and self-knowledge. There, on a hill overlooking a river, in a land redolent with memories beneath a swaying magnolia tree, my journey would end, just as it had done for my father the bleak afternoon in September, 22 years ago.

About The Author

Karim Raslan was born in Petaling Jaya, Selangor in 1963. Educated in both Malaysia and England, he is a graduate in English and Law from St Johns' College, Cambridge. Whilst at Cambridge, he edited the university's newspaper *Stoppress and Varsity* in the year it won *The Guardian/NUS Award for Best Student Newspaper*. Called to the Bar in Inner Temple, he spent some of his time in London writing leader editorials for *The Times* on north and southeast Asia.

He later returned to Kuala Lumpur where he practised in a large legal firm before leaving the profession to work on a novel which remains unfinished. After working for a few years as a freelance writer and editor for many newspapers, journals and magazines, including *The Business Times (Singapore)*, the *New Straits Times*, the *Far Eastern Economic Review*, *The Sun* and *Men's Review*, he returned to legal practice.

He now spends his time trying to balance his writing with the demands of his work which takes him on a regular basis to South Africa. In South Africa, he speaks and advises in seminars and conferences on the Malaysian paradigm of equity through growth and the New Economic Policy (NEP).